MODELLING MINIATURE FIGURES

MODELLING MINIATURE FIGURES

Edited by Bruce Quarrie

Patrick Stephens, Cambridge

First published — 1975
First softbound edition — 1978

ISBN 0 85059 331 X

Jacket photograph by Philip O. Stearns

Set in 9pt Plantin type and printed in Great Britain
on Clan Book Wove 90 gsm for the publishers,
Patrick Stephens Limited, Bar Hill, Cambridge, CB3 8EL,
by Blackfriars Press Limited of Leicester, and bound by
Hunter & Foulis Limited of Edinburgh.

Contents

SECTION ONE

Introduction

Most modellers today take plastic completely for granted, few of them realising quite what a revolution this much-maligned substance has wrought in the world of model figures over the last thirty years. Coming in a variety of guises, from soft, rubbery compounds of the PVC and polyethylene families to the more brittle polystyrene, plastic is undoubtedly the most widely used modelling material available today.

In the figure field its main significance lies in the way it has brought the model soldier into the pocket money bracket, for although the hollow-cast lead figures made by Britains have been widely available since the turn of the century, serious figures accurately depicting the men and uniforms of history were only available as expensive, solid-cast metal 'collectors' items until quite recently. Today, although the expensive metal figures still exist—and, indeed, continue to grow in popularity hand in hand with the growth of leisure and money to spend on leisure in Western society—the plastic figure has acquired an even greater following.

Due to the ease with which plastic, particularly the polystyrene variety, can be moulded into complex yet perfectly delineated shapes; and due to its relative cheapness (although the long-term effects of oil shortages and embargoes have yet to make themselves truly felt), plastic has emerged as an ideal substance for all forms of modelling. The result has been a massive influx of plastic model figures depicting the warriors—and civilians—of virtually every historical period, in both the traditional 54mm (1:32 scale) and the smaller 00/HO gauge (1:76 to 1:72 scale, or 20mm).

In the following chapters a selection of authors, all well-known in their respective fields, and many of them long-standing contributors to modelling publications such as *Scale Models, Airfix Magazine* and *Military Modelling,* discuss their own methods of tackling plastic figures in both scales. In some cases the ideas contradict one another, since every modeller evolves his own favourite way of tackling things. This does not mean that one is right and the other wrong. Modelling is an art, not a science, and different methods suit different temperaments.

In particular, you will find many different types of paint recommended, from the popular enamels to acrylics, posters and oils. Don't allow this to confuse you —experiment yourself with the different types and choose the one (or ones, since most of them can be mixed on a model in perfect harmony) which suits *you.*

And in other things too: do not take this book as an authoritative 'ten commandments' of figure modelling. There is no such thing. There are only techniques which suit the individual and the type of model he is trying to create. However, each of the authors in this book has had several years' model making experience, and each of the techniques, tools and materials advocated is the result of much trial-and-error experience which it would take the newcomer just as long to acquire.

Similarly, even if you do have several years' modelling experience yourself, don't sneer at someone else's technique until you've tried it yourself: it may produce a considerably better result, or at least save you a great deal of time and energy. There is nothing 'sinful' in short cuts. Modelling is supposed to be a hobby to bring you relaxation, not a penance, and there is no point in tackling things the hard way if a simpler course will bring about a comparable result.

However, there are certain basic items which any modeller working in plastic will require, and it would be as well to outline these now. The first is an adequate working surface. If you have your own den or workshop, all well and good, but most modellers find themselves forced to commandeer the dining room table, and consequently a firm working surface is essential. A sheet of thick ply or chipboard is ideal for this, since it will absorb saw and knife cuts, soldering iron burns and spilt paint easily without threatening domestic tranquillity. Similarly, a stout wooden, plastic or metal box in which to store paints, tools, scrap plastic, sprue, and all the other oddments which we modellers seem to attract around us is another essential.

So far as tools go, the main requisites are a selection of craft knives and razor blades or, if you can get them, a surgical scalpel and a selection of blades. But *please*, if there are small children in your family, do keep careful track of these and ensure they are always stored safely out of reach when not in use.

For major conversion work a razor saw or, if you can't afford one, a junior hacksaw, is also essential. Other than these, a pair of pointed-ended tweezers, scissors, a pair of dividers and a small vice are the only other essential tools.

If you are going to be doing a great deal of animation and conversion work, then it is well worth investing in a Pyrogravure, a precision tool rather like a miniature soldering iron, but with a variety of differently shaped tips. On the other hand, a small soldering iron will work almost as well for most jobs, and will also come in handy if you intend to tackle some figure conversions in metal as well as plastic. It is also useful for mending a variety of objects around the home!

Other useful tools include a small hand drill or pin drill, a selection of small files, and varying grades of sand or glasspaper.

Materials: well, apart from paints, which we have already discussed, you will want some brushes. And here I cannot stress too strongly—buy the most expensive you can possibly afford. This is one area where you really do get what you pay for, and a good sable hair brush will repay your investment many times over, whereas a cheap one will not only leave odd hairs in your immaculate paintwork but will probably become quite unusable in very short order.

The other materials you will need are adhesives, and the most sensible course is to have as wide a selection available as possible, ranging from normal polystyrene 'tube' cement through liquid polystyrene cement to impact adhesives such as Bostik and epoxy resins such as Britfix. Besides adhesives you will also require a body filler or plastic putty of some description. The choice here is vast, ranging from Humbrol customising body putty to plastic metal, but the best currently available—for reasons which several authors make clear in this book—is Squadron 'Green Stuff'. Other than this, you will require a selection of sheets of plastic card of varying thickness, plastic strip and rod, notepaper, tissue paper, and cotton. As you progress, and experiment, you will find other materials and tools you will wish to add to this list, but for the moment the above will do.

8

one

Robert C. Gibson
Small-scale plastic figures

In our first chapter, Robert Gibson, who has contributed several series of articles on modelling and converting 00/HO gauge plastic figures to Airfix Magazine, discusses the possibilities of animating and converting the wide variety of model figures in this handy scale, and shows how some very effective single figures and small dioramas can be constructed with a minimum of tools and experience. If you have never tried converting or modelling figures in plastic, it is probably a good idea to buy a couple of boxes of the cheap Airfix figures and try swopping a few heads, arms and legs around to see what you can produce. The techniques are similar to those required on larger figures, and if you muck up one figure, there are plenty more in the box!

Plastics came into everyday use in the late 1930s, and were given great impetus during the Second World War, yet it was not until the late 1950s that Airfix and Louis Marx entered the model soldier field with 20mm size figures. At that time, supplies of non-British plastic toys and kits were rather unsteady, so it is fair to say that the early Airfix plastic Guardsmen gave a tremendous boost to the pastime of wargaming in Britain, enabling many a potential wargamer to buy his first 'regiment' and convert it— all at a reasonable price compared with the specialist metal figure.

The quality of those early figures was nowhere near present-day standards; but it was certainly good enough to encourage both buyers and makers—further additions to the ranges were soon produced and as eagerly snapped up by the wargaming fraternity. Today, Airfix alone produce 46 different 'sets', eight of which are of a non-military nature—but are often used to provide the occasional unusual 'special' figure, eg army or navy officers in duffle coats, or Zulu warriors, or even Regimental mascots. Louis Marx are more difficult to assess, since the sets available in Britain are constantly changing, but their products have included Vikings, mediaeval warriors, German Second World War infantry and vehicles, and American Civil War soldiers.

Others have been swift to emulate the success of the 'founders'—more often than not copying their products—but a few are worth mention. Spencer-Smith figures are sold in bulk on the specialist wargame market; a larger scale is used— 30mm for foot figures and 26-27mm for cavalry—and the semi-flat style is rather reminiscent of the pre-1914 toy soldier. The quality is reasonable, but the uniform detail is a trifle indeterminate—Prussian Uhlans of 1814 being more appropriate to 1914!

In Italy, the firm of Atlantic now produce some excellent Airfix-style sets depicting modern Italian soldiers and parade sets of the Hitler and Mussolini eras. Quality is very good, but with a strictly limited number of action positions.

The spread in popularity of 00/HO tank kits brought polystyrene soldiers on to the market. Starting with Airfix's tank and gun crews, Almark have brought out two sets of British infantry, and Fujimi and Eidai from Japan have contributed to the rising interest in better Second World War figures (although the Eidai figures bear a striking resemblance to the original Airfix German Infantry set!). In 1:87 scale, Roco-Minitanks have produced some excellent modern and Second World War figures in polystyrene to complement their range of tanks and military vehicles.

Tools and materials

In order to make the best use of your figures, a number of tools will come in handy in preparing them for painting and in conversion work.

Cutting tools a modelling knife of normal size, with a selection of sharp blades (at least two of the most used variety to enable changing over if one blade snaps or goes blunt). Swann-Morton, X-Acto and Humbrol make suitable knives with a wide range of blades. A sharp double-edged razor blade is useful for exchange surgery, ie swopping heads, arms, etc, since the thin blade reduces distortion of the cut, and thus ensures a better subsequent fit. Scissors come in handy for cutting belts and webbing and flags from paper.

Other tools since most groups and horses mounted on scenic bases must be heat-sealed, a candle set in a jar lid or shallow tobacco tin comes in useful for heating the pin or old knife blade used for sealing (but do not use near thinners or enamel paint tins). An old paint brush with a reasonable amount of bristle left on it can be used to coat polythene (soft plastic) figures before painting.

Materials Plasticine is invaluable for adding extra clothing and blanket rolls. It can be 'fixed' for painting by covering with liquid polystyrene cement, Humbrol Banana Oil or Unibond glue. The Banana Oil is probably the best medium, since it can be brushed on and the brushes cleaned in white spirit or turps afterwards. Paper comes in very handy for all kinds of jobs —good quality writing paper, for instance, will make excellent webbing when cut into thin strips, and hard tissue paper, such as fruit is wrapped in, can be used for canvas covers, groundsheets, and home-made flags and lance-pennants. Thin stiff wire or pins are essential for the converter to support 'exchanged' heads, arms, etc, when cut into short lengths. Polystyrene cement is essential for polystyrene (ie hard plastic) figures, but is equally useful for polythene figures, where it can be used for securing paper webbing, filling gaps between new heads or limbs and their new body, and even coating Plasticine for painting. If Airfix extend the use of the new, hard, flexible plastic (currently being used on their 1:32 scale 'ready-made' vehicles) to their 00/HO figures, then polystyrene cement will be usable for cementing the figures as well. Banana Oil and the other 'fixatives' mentioned in connection with Plasticine are useful also for coating a figure prior to painting. Cotton wool, soaked with polystyrene cement, is a most useful material for manufacturing plumes, bearskins, busbies and sporrans. Other materials sometimes prove useful, eg scrap plastics of all kinds such as cocktail sticks. Even grass 'reeds' were successfully used to lengthen the barrel of the English Civil War musketeer in one of the photographs—converted from a Japanese infantryman suitably trimmed of equipment and with modified helmet.

Choosing a figure

If you intend to convert a figure to some other army or period, or even use a standard figure for a purpose for which it was not originally posed, there are three factors to be considered, viz: stance, dress, and weapons.

Stance is of the greatest importance: make sure it is physically possible for the man to be doing what you intend him to be doing. Some actions, eg bayonet charging, are difficult to change because the pose is so obviously that of thrusting with something. To change it to pulling on a rope, for example, the action must be literally reversed—fore leg straight, rear leg bent and body leaning back. If you have doubts on a pose, literally try it yourself, and see if it is possible. Wherever possible, get photographs or drawings of what you want to depict— these will often suggest a likely figure to you. If the arms or legs are not right, see if you can find the right ones—and change them.

Always remember to make sure the man is facing the right way—I can remember laboriously altering a 1914 German infantryman swinging his rifle to a dismounted Uhlan holding his horse—the trouble was that he remained facing stolidly ahead when he should have been looking towards the horse's head, and at what he was supposed to be doing. The question of stance is more important still if you intend to create a group of interacting figures, eg an artillery crew. In this case you will need to know something of the procedure for firing the gun in question: for an 18th or early 19th Century cannon, for example, to know that no person stood directly to the rear of the gun, because of the total recoil of the gun and carriage; and conversely, on a field gun of more modern times (ie after 1910), every member was placed in line behind the gun shield for protection against small arms fire and for ease of ammunition handling. Thus a Napoleonic gun crew would be standing and spread on either flank in action, while a 25 pounder crew would be kneeling (unless in indirect fire support, ie enemy not visible) to the rear of the gun shield or gun emplacement. In more detail, where a loading and ramming operation is taking place, the figure of the gunner firing the piece will need alteration . . . or omission.

Dress can be a very important factor in choosing the figure. It can make things easy (eg the dress of 18th Century infantry men varied largely in headdress and facing details—so the basic figures are to be found amongst the Airfix British Grenadiers or Washington's Army); or it can pose its own problems (eg for cavalry of the same period, there is no 'in-period' figure, so one has to take a closer look at other horsemen of other periods to see if they are suitable for conversion). In the modern periods of military dress, fashions sometimes change frequently, like the British Army battledress between 1914 and the present day; or remain basically the same, like the Russian tunic, trousers and jackboots which have remained essentially similar from 1900 to the present, thus enabling us with changes of heads to represent the Russian infantry of 1904-5, 1914-17 and 1939-45.

Not only clothes but hair styles are important here—the soldiers of the 1740 to 1800 period wore their hair long, gathered at the nape of the neck, and often

powdered; the soldiers of the 1890 to 1914 era wore it very short indeed, almost shaven, round the neck and ears—a fashion which continued to find favour in the Russian and German Armies until 1945, often in extreme forms. Some American paratroopers of the 82nd and 101st Airborne Divisions in June 1944 shaved their heads leaving only a central crest of hair, Red Indian fashion, and daubed their faces in red and white 'warpaint'. The simple moustache becomes important—prior to the Victorian era, it was very rare in the British Army except in foreign and rifle corps around 1800, yet it was compulsory in many German units of the 18th Century, to the extent of marking moustaches on the upper lips of those who could not grow them naturally. Contemporary illustrations or reliable modern references will help you in points of dress or coiffure.

Weapons are less important than the other factors, yet they can affect stance, where weapons are to be added or where a change of period is involved and a different arms drill is in use. In 00/HO scale, the vital factor for small arms is size—the difference between the bolt of a breechloading rifle and the firing mechanism of a muzzle-loading musket is less important than the right overall size—the two parts look much the same painted, but a shorter or longer weapon will ruin the whole effect of a figure. If you can find a hand clutching the appropriate Lee-Enfield or PPSh or MP40, well and good, but if not, look for one which is the same size and work from there.

Sometimes an absence of weapon makes all the difference. The Airfix Russian Infantry set contains a good marching figure which, with weapon removed, can be converted to less warlike poses. The German Hussar officer in undress cap, and the portrait figure of Manfred von Richthofen (the 'Red Baron') both originated from this figure after an exchange of heads and some carving and building work.

Converting

The converting of both polythene and polystyrene figures falls into four stages: first, trim—removing the moulding flash, trimming off small details and protruding items such as pouches and packs; second, alter—changing the length and thickness of garments, shapes of hats, trousers, etc (this can be a first step for stage four); third, exchange—swop heads, horses, arms, legs—or parts of arms or legs; and fourth, build up—add items like great-coats, packs, blankets and blanket rolls, loose weapons and tools.

It is generally a good practice, especially for beginners to converting, to work through the four stages in the order shown, missing out the unnecessary ones. As suggested, stage two (alter) can be a preliminary to stage four (build up) in changing from, say, a single-breasted tunic to a double-breasted greatcoat. In this case, the front of the tunic has to be smoothed off, and the belts and webbing may have to be removed. The short skirts of the tunic will have to be trimmed to suit the closer fit of the heavier and longer-skirted greatcoat below the belt (see Fig 1). Again, it is better to do de-

← *Greatcoat outline*

Fig 1

tailed carving before 'exchange' surgery is carried out, since the new part, whatever the plastic, will not be as secure. An exception to this might be where the removal of an original head or limb allows further carving to take place before the fitting of the new part—in this case, split stage three sensibly into two parts to allow further carving in between.

Trimming for all trimming work, a sharp modelling knife is essential. Preference in buying blades should be given to a straight-edged pointed blade, and a concave-edged blade for corner work. The broad blades are useful for big figures, but are of little use in this scale.

First, carefully remove the moulding 'flash', which forms a ridge right round the figure. Beware here of the figure which has suffered from bad mould register, and has two halves slightly out of alignment. If you can find another not so afflicted, do so—if not, proceed with extreme care when trimming, or build up the gap with Plasticine as described under 'building up'.

When trimming, make sure, especially with poor quality figures, that you do not remove items of equipment with the flash. If you are removing a pack from a soldier's back, do not forget to leave him with a reasonable back when you have finished —unless you are extracting a pack from a 'throwaway' figure for a stage three operation; likewise for the removal of belts, webbing and bayonets—leave what is underneath as it would be when the item taken is removed in real life. Sometimes this is not possible, for example with the engraved belts on the Airfix Confederate Infantry, where an application of stage four (building up), using Plasticine to fill up the engraved lines, and removing the excess with a knife, may be the solution instead.

Altering: this is an extension of the trimming operation, and is a more complex task: consider carefully before you pick up the knife what you are going to cut—and where.

The simplest of alterations is to give a trousered leg gaiters. The photographs show two examples, the Foreign Legionnaire of 1859, and the Irish Guardsman of 1903. The Legionnaire was selected from the Airfix Union Infantry set as being closest to the French infantry dress of 1859—not surprising since this was the model for the regulation US Army dress of the 1860-78 period. The legs being fully trousered, a shallow cut was made at the place where the top of the gaiters appeared, and the trouser leg whittled away upwards towards the cut. Then, after the top had been created, the foot and ankle were trimmed. Finally, the trouser overhang above the gaiter was rounded off. The lengthened tunic was created by cutting back the existing skirts and cutting new skirts lower down.

The Irish Guardsman was chosen from the First World War German Infantry with the help of a contemporary illustration of the 'Micks' on a route march. Only the gaiters posed any serious problem— they were shorter than the German boot, but fortunately the trousers above the boot were gathered in a series of creases, enabling the boot to trouser join to become another crease—the gaiter being cut in the same fashion as that of the Legionnaire from the boot itself. (Note: the German style field cap worn, known as the Brodrick or Broderick cap, was little used by the British Army, except by the Irish Guards 1900-05, and the Royal Marine Light Infantry from about 1900 to 1914.)

Sometimes a small alteration will effect a change in type. The Airfix French Cuirassier can be easily changed to a French (mounted) Carabinier by removing the horse hair streamer on the helmet, and fitting a 'caterpillar' fur crest at stage four. The same alteration will also produce Bavarian Garde du Corps of 1814-15, both Cuirassier Regiments of the Kingdom of Westphalia 1808-14—the difference being created in the final painting of the figure and horse—and with a sabretache and minor stage one trimming, the British Life Guards and Royal Horse Guards of 1815. The possibilities of this conversion should underline the need for checking dress when choosing a figure—basic dress, ie short coatee, 'Roman' helmet, breeches and high boots, and basic horse furniture, is the same for all of these. A simple conversion makes it possible, and painting makes the difference between the conversions.

Exchanges the simplest exchanges are those which involve no cutting: for example, an Airfix Royal Horse Artillery driver or officer can be remounted on a British Hussar's horse to create that much-neglected cavalryman, the pre-1812 British Light Dragoon, or even, with further work, a French Chasseur a Cheval of 1794-6.

First and most frequent of the types of exchange surgery are changes of head. This is often very effective: the three Prussian Foot Guards in the photographs were simple exchanges of Airfix First World War German heads on to Guards Colour Party bodies. The removal of the bearskin-clad head requires careful razor blade work, and still leaves a certain amount of trimming to be done to finally clean the rifle away from the flash on the shoulder.

Further examples of this are as follows. Add the head of a British First World War infantryman to the body of a Russian infantryman to produce a Russian First World War infantry figure; a British 8th Army head with a British First World War infantry body produces a late First World War British (basic); a French Cuirassier head plus British Grenadier body gives 1780 British Light infantry (basic); while a Washington's Army head on a French Cuirassier body produces a Prussian, Austrian or French 18th Century Cuirassier (basic).

Additional work would be needed on the last three—marked (basic)—for example, gas-mask satchels for the late First World War British, shorter coat tails and a lower helmet crest for the 1780 Light Infantry, small sabretaches for the Prussians and small details for the other cuirassiers, but the major change in appearance has been effected, and now the polishing and perfecting can begin.

Of course, no two conversions by head exchange need look alike, and if you are constructing a diorama, for example, it may be highly undesirable. The two infantrymen of 1685 in the photograph were constructed for a Monmouth Rebellion period diorama not yet completed: the basis was the French First World War infantryman with rifle at ease, chosen for 'stance', and the head came from the slouch-hatted Confederate infantry whose hats were of similar style to 1685 fashions. The cut on the neck was made so that the head could rotate evenly and naturally—thus two different figures were born, chatting amiably on campaign awaiting orders. The same operation could have been undertaken with Union infantry with kepis to create two equally garrulous French 'poilus' of 1914-15.

The above conversion raises a very important point in exchange surgery, ie that the cut must be straight and level, so that the new part fits as if it belonged there in the first place. An uneven cut will result in a bad fit—a thin double-edged razor blade is best for this operation, since a thick blade will move the item being cut off and give a distorted cut (see Fig 2). Do not try V-shaped cuts unless you have a lot of spares: it is infinitely more difficult to get a good fit by this method than by the straight cut method, and in 99 per cent of cases is not worth the effort.

Arm swopping can produce a position missed by the manufacturer—for example, the Airfix French Cuirassiers lack a trumpeter. The Guards Band trumpet is

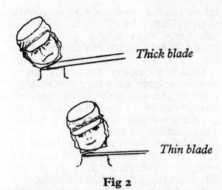

Thick blade

Thin blade

Fig 2

the right length, so the right arm and trumpet are removed, and the right arm of a Cuirassier including the epaulette is removed. A new epaulette is carved from the upper part of the trumpet arm, and both arm and body are drilled with a pin for the fitment of a short length of stiff wire to join new arm to new body. When the wire is inserted, first in the body then the arm fitted over it, the arm can be fixed with the trumpet in any desired position, ready for use or at rest, as shown in the photograph. The same operation can be used to fit an arm grasping a rifle—the Australian Light Horse trooper has a Confederate slouch hat and a new arm fitted to a US Civil War Artillery rider's body, with lengthened tunic and boots added at stage two by judicious carving.

Building up at this stage, we have usually completed the basic figure, and all that remains is for the small touches of detail that add authenticity to a figure to be added—a slung blanket roll round a Prussian soldier brought back from 1914 to 1870, or a haversack on a Washington's Army infantryman to make him one of Frederick the Great's musketeers (incidentally, one of the simplest conversions of all except painting—and shown in the photographs).

The best materials for building up are paper and Plasticine. Writing paper cannot be bettered for creating belts— cut into long parallel strips it can be fitted in position and then cut off after cementing in place. Hard tissue paper is most useful for flags, lance pennons and groundsheets—although there is another method of doing this mentioned later.

Plasticine is invaluable for all the softer outlines, eg haversacks, blanket rolls, the baggy smock shown on the German paratrooper in the photograph (whose smock was lengthened with Plasticine to give the odd short-legged look typical of the average wearer of the Fallschirmjager jump smock). When using Plasticine, coat it with one of the 'fixatives' before painting.

A very effective method of producing plumes and 'furry' items is to use ordinary cotton wool, roughly trimmed to size and rolled into shape, then soaked in polystyrene cement. The result is light in weight, and easily affixed to the figure (in the case of plumes). For complex structures such as the Crimean period 93rd Highlander's feather bonnet, a pin is used to support the cotton wool itself, and allow 'modelling' of the bonnet to take place on the head.

Fine stiff wire is most useful for lances and flagstaffs, since it can, with prior drilling, be inserted into the hand to form a sound mechanical joint, not easily broken. Heat stretched sprue can also be used, and indeed, may be preferable where the lance is not held, but slung from the arm or shoulder. Sprue is not really suitable for flag staffs, however, since the flag has to be fixed by cementing along over 40 per cent (at least) of the staff's length: stretched sprue is easily weakened or, worse still, melted by too much polystyrene cement.

As mentioned above, flags and lance pennons are usually fashioned out of paper, and painted on the staff in the desired position for realism. In recent years, however, use has been made of fine draughting linen of the type intended for drawing offices. This material can be soaked to remove most of the starch which gives it its bluish colour; after ironing, it provides a first class medium for producing flags.

Briefly, the technique is as follows: mark out and paint the flag itself (both sides) using a waterproof-drying poster colour such as Pelikan Plaka, cut out the flag and enough extra to fix it to the staff, and after cementing securely, dampen the flag and bend carefully into position, holding it there until dry. There should be sufficient starch left in the material to retain it in position when properly dry. Fringes can be created, prior to painting, by unpicking the threads next to the outside edge of the flag. Alternatively, there are a number of ready-printed stick-on flags produced by model transfer manufacturers such as Almark.

Polystyrene figures can be modified using much the same materials as for polythene figures—remembering, of course, that sparing use should be made of polystyrene cement to avoid damage to the figure. Some of the 'hard' plastic figures currently available (eg Roco-Minitanks tank commanders and Fujimi figure sets), have separate arms which enable a fair degree of 'customisation' to be obtained.

Painting

It is probably fair to say that painting itself is of secondary importance to the preparation of the figure for painting. No amount of painting skill can redeem a badly prepared figure.

By converting or merely trimming our figure we have completed the first and most essential part of the preparation. To the figure a good undercoat of matt white enamel is applied thinly overall. When dry, the figure can be examined for flaws in carving or conversion (eg the join of lengthened coat tails can be examined to see if the join is too obvious) and any remedial action necessary can now be taken. Once we have satisfied ourselves that the figure is all it should be, we can proceed to the selection of the paint we want to use. The choice will be guided by three things: the type of paints we use; the colour range we possess; and the colours needed for the figure.

First, what kind of paints to use? Provided the figure is properly under-coated as above, we can use whatever paints we please. I have successfully used plastic enamels of all kinds in the past, and now use Pelikan Plaka casein-based poster paint. This gives a much richer range of colours for Napoleonic and earlier uniforms, and the use of matt and gloss polyurethane varnish over this gives semi-gloss and gloss finishes where needed. Others have just as successfully used oil-bound poster paints—the choice is up to your pocket and the availability of the paint.

Secondly, the range of colours will affect our choice—we may need to mix all our colours, or be able to find all of them ready from tin or jar. Flesh colour, despite the provision of ready-mixed colours, is best mixed when required. For example, an approximate 40 per cent white, 40 per cent yellow ochre (sand) and 20 per cent scarlet will provide a good basic European flesh colour, which can be toned by small additions of green or Prussian blue. A lighter colour (eg white) can be added to highlight nose, chin and forehead, and a touch of black added to the mix enables you to shadow eye sockets, the area under the chin and either side of the bridge of the nose.

The colours needed for the figure may affect the type or make of paints in the first place (ie we may buy paints to enable us to paint a given type of figure). For example, if we are likely to be painting a wide variety of uniform colours—Napoleonic uniforms are a good example—it may be better to opt for gouache or poster colour paints, which give a considerable range of colours and shades not available in plastic enamels. Remember also that colour shades for the smaller figure should be a shade lighter than the mix for, say, a comparable 54 mm figure. This 'scale effect' is probably more demonstrable on model aircraft (eg Sea Grey Medium on a 1:32 scale aircraft looks much lighter than on the same aircraft in 1:72 scale).

Brushes are very important—do not use any brush where the bristles no longer come to a point. Try to buy the best—sable hair if you can afford it, squirrel hair if you cannot—but never buy brushes which do not identify the 'hair' used. The good quality brushes last longer—and longer still with frequent cleaning in soap and water. Six months' use with

Table of basic flesh colour mixes

Type	Ground colour mix	Highlight with	Shadow with
European (blonde)	White, yellow ochre, scarlet and a touch of green	Mix + white	Mix + brown
European (dark)	White, yellow ochre, scarlet and a touch of Prussian blue	Mix + light grey	Mix + black
American Indian	White and red-brown with ten per cent brown	Mix + white	Mix + brown
Oriental	White and red-brown with ten per cent yellow	Mix + white	Mix + red brown
Negroid	White and brown with five per cent black	Mix + white	Mix + black

plastic enamels, and two to four years' use with poster colours are normal in my experience.

Always start by painting the face and hands—whether you go down to the detail of marking in individual eye pupils or just marking an eyebrow line, no other surface will offer so much difficulty, and so much chance of splashing unwanted paint elsewhere as the face.

First, mix a basic medium face colour —see table.

These are all basic colours, and may need revision for your particular soldier. For example, the inhabitants of some parts of southern and central India have a very dark skin pigmentation, requiring extra quantities of both blue and black mixed with the Negroid basic mix. The Gurkha soldier is of an Oriental rather than an Indo-European race, and would require the appropriate mix. The majority of northern India's ethnic groups would require a European (dark) mix.

Always line the eyes with black: in this scale, if the pupil is to be marked, do this also in black. When the face and hair have been painted and have dried, varnish over-all with a good matt polyurethane varnish: this will protect the tiny details, and give the face and hair a 'live' appearance.

Once the face is painted, start to work outwards on the rest of the uniform. Collar and cuffs are best painted next, together with anything else near face and hands; leave boots and headgear until last. Avoid highlighting in painting uniforms in this scale (unless you can produce subtle variations only just lighter than the original shade), but use plenty of shadow—see Fig 3. Good use of shadow will produce a figure that will stand out in its own right—no matter how small.

Avoid the use of gloss varnish for leatherwork and horses—matt polyurethane varnish will give the correct amount of sheen at this scale. If you have to protect the figure against handling (eg for wargames use) use the matt polyurethane varnish overall. A warning, though —if you are using metallic enamels, do not varnish over them or they may smear; if you are using poster colour metallics such as Plaka, you can varnish over in complete safety. If in doubt, find out by experiment on a piece of scrap, not on your nearly completed figure!

Artillery

Often, the boxes of 00/HO soldiers we buy contain small artillery pieces— indeed, a few are specifically designed and

Horses

The following Table gives a useful guide to painting horses:

Type	Colours
Light Bay*	Body reddish-brown. Mane, tail and legs below knee black.
Dark Bay*	Body dark brown, otherwise as light bay.
Light Chestnut*	Body yellow-brown or reddish-brown (more usual) and legs of the same colour. Mane and tail slightly lighter.
Liver Chestnut*	Body dark brown and legs similar. Mane and tail yellow-brown or reddish-brown.
Brown*	Very dark brown or black all over. Nose brown.
Grey*	Off-white or cream with grey dapple, mostly on neck and flanks varying in degree from horse to horse. Legs below knee grey. Mane and tail grey or white.
Blue Roan*	Grey with black dapple. Mane and tail black. Legs below knee black or very dark grey.
Black*	Black all over.
White	Off-white all over or white all over.
Dun	Dun body, black legs, mane and tail and stripe down spine (mainly a pony colour, eg Cossack ponies).
Piebald	White, with irregular patches of black. Mane and tail are the same colour as the adjacent portion of neck and rump.
Skewbald	As piebald, but reddish-brown or dark-brown over white.
Strawberry Roan	Reddish-brown dappled with grey, maximum grey on upper surfaces. Legs dark brown. Mane and tail grey.

*All horses marked thus are liable to have white markings on face and legs below ankle. The face marking, called a 'blaze' can be large or small. Few horses have no blaze, likewise few have no 'socks' on the legs or on all four legs—one or two is normal.

For further details on horse modelling and animation, see Chapter 11.

Airfix 00/HO polythene figure conversions by Robert Gibson. **Above** Two Prussian 7 Years' War figures, Crimean Highlander, German para-trooper and two Jacobean soldiers. **Right** French cuirassiers altered to provide different figures. Two trumpeters with arms borrowed from the Guards Band set and a Carabinier with cotton wool crest. **Below right** American Civil War gun team. **Bottom** more of the conversions described in Chapter 1: hussar in undress cap, Manfred von Richthofen, Foreign Legionnaire, Irish Guardsman and three Prussian Foot Guards.

Above *Modern Italian infantrymen —
Bersaglieri, Alpini and parachutists, all
from the Atlantic range in 00/HO scale.*
Left *Robert Gibson's effective little '1812'
diorama using converted Airfix figures.*
Bottom *two views of Sid Horton's SS
Cavalry trooper.*

Top *Two more views of Sid Horton's SS Cavalry figure converted from Airfix 'Collector's Series' kit parts.* **Right** *Another of Sid Horton's figures. This represents a Frankish warrior of approximately 400 AD and was based on the Airfix Highlander figure. The basic figure's sleeves were carved into arms as shown, the skirt, belt and sword sling made from 5 thou plastic card, the hair, fur jerkin and shoes built up from Squadron Green Putty, axe and sword from laminated plastic card, and the shield from a plastic table-tennis ball, cut out with a pair of dividers.*

Above *Posed resting on the wing of a Spad XIII, Bill Hearne's First World War aviator's posture lends itself to many interesting possibilities. Infusing an air of relaxation into an animation can prove difficult because not only must the body position express, but also the clothing must be planned and worked to convey the desired impression.* **Left** *The same figure posed leaning against the cowling of a Nieuport Scout. Here you can see how the various radiations of creases and folds in the clothing add to the posture and help in the creation of a very realistic vignette.*

Fig 3

class model, and compare it with the kit.

Secondly, when you want to modify it to some other type of gun, gather all the material you can lay hands on covering the gun to be modelled. Books, drawings and photographs will all help to produce a realistic, if not necessarily 100 per cent accurate model. Do not strive too hard to make a perfect model first time off—the object of a hobby is to enjoy doing it, not make hard work for yourself!

Thirdly, when you get down to carving, be careful! A little pressure on the blade may go a long way—and guns are comparatively expensive to replace as against figures—there are rarely more than two per set.

The materials that will come in most useful here are scrap plastic and 'spares', and good notepaper. Scrap plastic will enable the addition of buckets, rammers, ammunition boxes, etc; the 'spares' box can provide wheels, barrels and carriages, especially for the more modern weapons. Notepaper will enable you to add simulated ironwork to the carriage (with 'spots' of polystyrene cement as rivets) and reinforcing bands to the barrels. A heated pin will serve to 'bell out' the muzzle where this becomes necessary (see Fig 4).

Painting guns and ancillary equipment such as limbers and ammunition caissons requires colour information—below is a table of colours for the popular Napoleonic period.

Barrels were brass or iron—in the latter case the actual colour was often that of black lead. There were exceptions to the patterns given below, and even contemporary artists were not always scrupulously accurate in painting the 'guns', but by and large the table is a good guide to 'how shall I paint it?'.

grouped round the 'guns'. To describe how to convert and paint 00/HO artillery is not really within the scope of this book, but a few pointers as to how to set about it may not come amiss.

First, never assume your 'gun' cannot be improved on—it can usually be brought up to 'operational' standard by simple additions made from wire and scrap plastic. Find an illustration of the real thing to assist you—or failing that, a first

Table of gun carriage colours

Country	Wooden parts	Metal fittings
Britain	Medium blue-grey	Black
France	Dark/medium green	Black
Prussia	Light blue	Black
Russia	Dark (bottle) green (1814-Medium blue-grey)	Black
Austria	Chrome yellow	Black
Bavaria	Light grey	Black
Hesse-Darmstadt	Medium blue	Black
Baden	Dark grey	Black
Saxony	Dark grey	Yellow
Wurttemberg	Natural wood	Yellow
Denmark	Red	Yellow
Sweden	Bluish-green	Black or yellow
Naples	Light blue	Black

*Writing paper strips
and cement blob 'rivets'*

Writing paper strips

Fig 4

Dioramas

The 00/HO plastic figure, by virtue of its cheapness, size and convertibility is ideally suited to diorama work, but too often we see dioramas in this scale ruined by poor execution of a sound original idea. The usual failures are the overcrowding of figures, poor painting of the figures themselves, and poor representation of terrain.

Overcrowding is something everyone does at first—the appeal of massed cavalry against squares of infantry fires us all, then one day we get away from the general histories and start to read of the exploits of individual soldiers, and we absorb more detail of what it was like to be 'there'. At this point, many a good diorama is born—the 42nd Highlanders at Quatre Bras, for example: really not a regimental battle, but a mass of individual struggles against the French Lancers of Pire's Division, which can be shown by a smaller group on both sides, the long corn stalks adding to the dramatic effect.

The small dioramas in the photographs show how effective 'small groups' can be. '1812' depicts the French retreat from Moscow in the winter of that year. There is no need to include the Russians—the wounded and the dying are evidence enough, as are the levelled muskets of the untidy firing line. The real enemy, winter, is visible on the ground, on their clothes, and fast covering the dead and dying.

'Gettysburg 1863' shows a good subject for a small diorama, namely a gun crew in action. Having modelled an Armstrong breech-loading cannon from the Airfix US Civil War 'Napoleon' gun, I wanted to display the gun at work. The original diorama was overcrowded with figures—nine in all—but after further consideration of the role, possible crew of a solitary Armstrong in this action (and the acquisition of a lot more data on the period), the number of figures was drastically reduced, the remaining figures repainted and the terrain improved.

Poor painting—what can we say? Do not attempt too many figures at once, and take your time over them. A few well-painted figures are worth a host of colourful rubbish. Use matt paints for figures and scenery: paint the figures before fixing in the diorama, with the possible exception of headgear.

Terrain can be a real problem. If you have chosen a historical (ie real) setting, study illustrations of it. Do not forget that the season of the year will affect the colour and presence of leaves on trees, ice on streams and puddles, and mud on roads, soldiers' boots, and just about everything else in range (having said that —do not overdo it—and remember there is wet mud and dry mud, and numerous permutations in between). If you use scenic grasses and trees, remember to check for scale—lichen at 54mm may be little larger than a cabbage, whereas at 00/HO scale it can provide good cover for a soldier.

When building a diorama, keep your men and equipment separate, and, as far as possible do all necessary work on them before placing them in their final positions. Make as many 'dry runs' as you like before painting to check stance, position, etc, but once painted, keep them aside until you are ready to incorporate them in the scene.

Once in position, the terrain is built up round the bases until they disappear. If the base is too thick or is unnecessary, remove all or part of it: 'baseless' figures can be pinned on to the base after foot positions are marked, and short lengths of stiff wire or pins let into the base board. This method can also be used for very small scenic groups such as the gun crew in the photographs.

For further hints on making dioramas, see Chapter 12.

two

Roy Dilley
54mm figures in polythene

In this second chapter, Roy Dilley, the president of the British Model Soldier Society, takes up Robert Gibson's theme and describes how similar techniques can be applied to the animation and conversion of soft plastic (ie polythene and PVC) figures in 54mm or 1:32 scale. Although he has concentrated on the range of figures manufactured by Britains (which now includes a lively selection of models from the popular Napoleonic period) the methods discussed are equally applicable to the figures made by firms such as Timpo or Airfix in this type of material.

Much of what I have said in a later chapter concerning their metal models applies equally to the plastic products of Britains Ltd. Scale, proportion, and design are kept more or less constant in the same way, and, if anything, the engraving and sculpture are generally superior to that of the hollow-cast lines. Since the issue of Britains' plastic items commenced some years after the Second World War, the materials used in their production have always been flexible plastics of the unbreakable type, at first polythene, but latterly poly-vinyl-chloride or PVC. Polythene has a number of disadvantages when used as the base material for model figures, chief among them being the tendency of thin sections to become easily distorted, the scuffed and fibrous condition to which the surface area deteriorates with time and rough handling, and the inability of that surface to accept and retain paint without very rapid flaking and shredding. From the converter's point of view the substance becomes even more intractable, bonding by means of adhesive alone is all but impossible, all joins made in this way needing some sort of added reinforcement, and all surfaces must be covered with a neutral film before painting can be accomplished with any lasting effect. Furthermore, polythene cannot satisfactorily be filed or sanded, all reduction having to be done by clean cutting and trimming with a very sharp blade. However, many interesting and unusual designs have been turned out in this stubborn material, some of which will be attractive to the converter, and if the right procedures are followed acceptable results can be achieved.

PVC on the other hand, is far more amenable both as to paint acceptance and retention, and bonding characteristics. Special PVC adhesives, such as those marketed by Humbrol and Helmet Products, enable bonds of considerable tenacity to be made without the necessity for pinning, and, provided the surface is cleaned by immersion in a detergent solution, paints of most kinds will adhere quite firmly. On the debit side, the flexible nature of this plastic does, like that of polythene, have the drawback of causing thin sections, rifle-barrels, sword-blades and scabbards and the like, to warp at the slightest provocation, a very irritating trait to the converter. Fortunately this adverse quality can be rectified, as will be explained later, and PVC can be carved and sanded, provided a fine grain paper is used. Epoxy adhesives too are fairly effective for bonding metal items to PVC, but the ketone, acetone, and chloroform based types are not satisfactory, as in the case of metal, but nonetheless, styrene, paper, cloth and so on can be used in conversion with the epoxies. Where a number of dissimilar materials have been utilised in a particular conversion, I make absolutely sure of a good painting surface by coating the entire model with a 'white' glue, Unibond, Elmers, Durofix, or some other similar PVA adhesive. This dries to a thin but tough overall skin, binding all added material firmly to the main mass without obscuring detail. Such 'white' glues are the neutral films with which I also coat polythene models, but they must be applied in these cases with care and patience to ensure that no areas, however small, are left uncovered to the subsequent detriment of the painting process. It cannot be too much emphasised that a sound painting surface is essential in all modelling, and it is well worth the trouble involved in preparing subjects in which flexible plastics are concerned to avoid the disappointment, not to say chagrin of having the paint job on a favourite piece disintegrate after a very short while.

As with plastic modelling generally, no elaborate tools are required to work the flexible materials, the main requisites being a very sharp craft-knife or scalpel, with separate blades that can be changed frequently to ensure the maintenance of a keen edge, a fine razor saw or piercing saw, tweezers, and fine grain sandpaper or emery-boards, the types used for manicure work being ideal, and a selection of drills and pin-chucks. Cloth, paper, styrene-sheet, strip and rod, cotton thread, wire, metal shims and foils, and small metal accessories, heads, equipment etc, can all be used with great success in this type of conversion, by making use of the bonding agents I have described above. In the case of polythene items, large sections, heads, arms, equipment and so on can be welded to one another by means of a heated blade applied to melt the surfaces together. Obviously some practice is advisable with this technique in order that the right amount of heat and the best manner of administering it can be judged with precision. This 'welding' process can also be employed to fill in large gaps or to build up areas which can later be carved into their final shapes, but, I must emphasise, the skill is one which takes some while to perfect, and should not be attempted unless you have a fair number of figures that you are willing to sacrifice in the cause of experience!

Probably the most satisfactory way of joining polythene parts is to pin them together with small lengths of dressmakers' pins or other types of wire, pressing the two plastic parts tightly against one another, with about half of the metal wire embedded into each. The join can then be reinforced by the welding technique, or by the use of epoxy adhesives. Where large areas are to be joined it may be necessary to use more than one pin in the joint, both to give added strength and to prevent any subsequent rotation or movement of the joined parts. The unfortunate tendency of some thin sections to become distorted can be counteracted by the insertion of a wire armature into the offending part. This process will require a hole to be drilled down the length of the item, rifle, sword scabbard or similar, before the armature, and a pin or portion of stiff wire pushed into place. If such rectification is not possible owing to the unsuitability of the part by reason of excessive thinness or length, then it is best to replace it entirely with a metal, hard plastic or 'scratch-built' piece of a rigid nature. It may well be desirable to pin such a replacement part to the polythene to be sure of a permanent union.

Provided the work is carried out with care and precision, very gratifying results can be achieved, and the finished model can, as it were, be 'shrunk' together by the application of an overall coat of 'white' glue. Think of the problems encountered when working with polythene as challenges to be met and overcome rather than as insurmountable obstacles, because a great many excellently designed figures, full of potential for conversion, can only be obtained in this awkward material, and it would be a pity not to make use of them merely because such usage is not all easy going.

PVC in thin sections also has a habit of warping, as has already been stated, but this can be dealt with in the same way as for polythene. Pinning may also be needed to reinforce joints which may be subjected to more than ordinary strain or pressure, but in the main, the material can be worked with reasonable facility, and bonds quite well with other substances. Sanding should be done very gently, with fine grain papers or emeryboards, and carving and cutting must be clean and precise, and be used in preference to sanding where considerable amounts of material are to be removed. A final pre-painting coat of 'white' glue is also desirable to hold everything more firmly together, and to provide a good surface for painting. Such extremely detailed and convincing pieces can be produced by the conversion of standard PVC models.

Britains do not issue figures made in the hard, 'rigid' plastics, polystyrene and the like, but have utilised them for certain of their model vehicles and buildings. They are docile materials from a conversion point of view, and can be cut, carved, sawn, filed, sanded, and bonded with much the same facility as metal, provided that the appropriate solvent or cement is used.

Whilst not as all embracing as those issued in metal, Britains' ranges of plastic models are sufficiently varied to provide a vast conversion potential. Basic figures cover a number of periods from ancient times to the present, including mediaeval, Napoleonic, American Civil War, and the Wild West, and there are comprehensive collections of animals, domestic and otherwise in the farm and zoological series. It is therefore possible to depict a surprising number of military and civilian types with only a minimum of conversion, whilst the constant scale and good proportional dimensions of the pieces allow really complex work to be undertaken without undue difficulty. The basic rules of anatomy, proportion, and balance are, of course, just the same as for metal figures, one's eye needs to be just as keen to spot conversion potential,

and one's imagination as lively to take the fullest advantage of what is available, whilst completed models can be displayed with metal items and be virtually indistinguishable from them.

Let us now consider a couple of actual examples, one simple, the other more complex, in which the practice of techniques will serve to give a sound idea of what will usually be involved when working in this medium. In neither case can a standard commercial model be obtained of the type depicted.

Conversion 1

This represents a soldier of the French Foreign Legion, serving in the Moroccan campaigns of the early 'twenties of this century, and utilises as a base figure the kneeling Japanese rifleman in the 'Deetail' series, Catalogue No 7352. The figure was first removed from its metal stand and had its detachable right arm unplugged and put on one side for the while. A really sharp knife or scalpel was used to pare off all moulding flash and tool marks, great care being taken not to cut into the model itself and damage detail. Next the haversack and waterbottle were cut from the rear of the figure, and the helmet was carved and sanded down to the plain cylindrical shape of the French kepi. A fine slot was made in the forehead with a razor saw, and a small piece of plastic card was cemented in to serve as the peak of the kepi. Having been sanded smoothly to shape, the water-bottle and haversack were reattached to the rear of the figure, their positions being reversed, ie the haversack now resting on the left hip, and with a short length of plastic rod inserted into the water-bottle to give it the characteristic 'bidon' style. The rifle was then cut completely away from the right arm, being replaced with a metal item (I used an HR Lebel rifle, but a similar piece could be filed down from a hard plastic weapon like those in the Almark series, or scratchbuilt from wire and scraps of card), then the arm and rifle were cemented back to the figure. It was then only necessary to attach a packaging ribbon rifle-sling before re-fixing the figure to its base and coating the whole item with PVA glue in readiness for painting. If desired a 'couvre-nuque' or neck curtain can be fitted, tissue-paper or very fine linen being suitable for this, but the Legion tended not to make much use of this protection in the years following the First World War.

Conversion 2

This is to depict a British General Officer in the order of dress known as 'Staff in Blues', circa 1914, and makes use of the old pattern mounted Confederate Officer from the ACW 'Eyes Right' series, (the new 'Deetail' figure of the same type, Catalogue No 7439, will do for this, but needs more extensive alteration), plus the Percheron Horse No 2106 in the Farm series, a Rose Models metal head, and various bits and pieces of plastic, wire, and ribbon from the spares box.

The conversion was commenced by cleaning off all mould marks and flash from the Percheron horse and the figure, the head of which was discarded. Then the holster and valise were trimmed from the ACW saddle, which was cemented into place on the horse's back, with a girth strap added from packaging ribbon. At this stage a length of brass wire, sharpened to a point at both ends, was inserted to half its length into the horse's back, through the centre of the saddle seat, leaving the remainder projecting vertically. A bridle was built up, again from ribbon, on the horse's head, with double cheek straps, nose and brow bands, and head and neck straps. This is the standard military bridle, in all respects similar to that moulded on the 'Eyes Right' horse. A piece of fuse wire, bent to shape and cemented into the mouth of the horse, served as a bit. All buttons were then trimmed from the man's coat front, and his legs were carved to represent breeches and riding-boots of the 'butcher' type worn in the British service. The arms and hands were trimmed plain, the sword being completely removed, and were then firmly cemented into place. Next, short lengths of wire were pushed into the heels of the figure to make spurs, and some Airfix plastic stirrups (from the Scots Grey kit) were found in the spares box and attached with ribbon 'leathers' to the boots. Ribbon sash ends and sword slings were then fitted, PVC adhesive held these quite firmly, and the Rose metal head No B155, with cocked hat, the feathers of which had been lengthened (with epoxy putty, 'Plastone' or 'Das'), was epoxied into the neck cavity. The sword, a Historex mameluke curved sabre with the scabbard trimmed smooth, was next attached to the slings before the man was joined to the horse by gently pushing him down on to the pin protruding from the saddle and securing with a dab of PVC adhesive. Reins, packaging ribbon again, were then made and fitted to the bit, and were brought back to be cemented to the figure's left hand, and the model was ready for coating preparatory to painting. In this conversion it will be noted that a number of dissimilar materials have been employed to get the effect, yet when painted they all blend happily together.

Try these examples, and make up others using your own imagination, and you will soon acquire the skills and techniques that will enable you to make use of whatever materials are available and best suited to your conversion requirements. Reference to the 'spares box' leads me to emphasise the point that, wherever possible, any parts of a figure or kit which have not been used in the finished model should not be thrown away, but be carefully preserved against any future needs. A well stocked spares box can save a great deal of trouble and exasperation if it can provide a part that could otherwise only be obtained by scratchbuilding.

It is my hope that readers of the foregoing will realise that the plastic figures of Britains Ltd are not to be dismissed as just 'toys', but can in fact provide the basic parts for truly accurate and artistic conversions of connoisseur quality.

three

Bill Hearne & Sid Horton
54mm scale collectors' models

The most outstanding development in the model soldier field as a result of the widespread availability of plastic after the Second World War was the introduction of the superb range of French-made 54mm figure kits by Historex. Each figure in this range is a genuine work of art, and the kits can be built up straight from the packet into masterpieces which would grace any museum display or collector's shelf. In this chapter Bill Hearne, well-known for his excellent modelling articles in Scale Models *and* Military Modelling, *describes his own methods of tackling Historex kits, and gives step-by-step instructions for two superb conversion projects.*

Following in Historex's footsteps, Airfix recently launched the first figures in a range of comparable—though much cheaper—54mm model figure kits. These are completely compatible with Historex, parts from both manufacturers being easily inter-mixable, and have brought the polystyrene figure kit within the 'pocket money' bracket. In the second half of this chapter Sid Horton, whose 'Charge of the Light Brigade' conversions in Airfix Magazine *have won universal acclaim, demonstrates some of his own techniques in modelling an SS cavalryman.*

The Historex and Airfix kits together are undoubtedly the most versatile and easily worked sources for the model figure maker today. The wealth of fine detail would have seemed impossible only a few years ago, and the quality of some of the conversions now seen at British Model Soldier Society meetings and other exhibitions has to be seen to be believed. Every figure modeller worth his salt should have a go at one of these superlative kits at least once, and those who have already tried assembling a kit in its 'straight from the packet' form will probably like to have a go at one of the conversions featured here. Nothing ventured, nothing gained.

When I decide upon making a particular model I endeavour to gather as much information and reference as possible before setting out on the project. I find it quite disturbing to complete a subject and then unearth some unquestionably authoritative material pertinent to it which indicates that I've committed an error or errors in equipment or uniform. Unfortunately it has been my experience to come across some grossly erroneous information in publications which claim to be the very ultimate word on some given subject, so one has to be exceedingly careful to double check and check again.

My other consideration is the animation which is something that I believe needs to be well thought out and settled upon before work is commenced. My approach here is to visualize a 'situation' in which the subject could be logically found: anything ranging from passive to highly active but giving the impression that although a single foot figure or a mounted one, the figure is part of a larger scene of activity. This is different, of course, from the individual model standing alone to display little more than uniform colour and detail and intending no more than that. On the basis of my concept much of this broader aspect of atmosphere is governed by another important factor, the foundation, base and/or groundwork upon which the model will be mounted. It is this relatively tiny area along with the attitude of the subject which will stimulate the imagination—or at least, that is what we hope—of a viewer. It's a good thing to remember that the groundwork and base constitutes the 'setting' for your figure which has taken hours to create and which, I feel certain, you would not wish to see marred by thoughtless or shoddy, unreal 'framing'. The base on which you stand your model is as important and as demanding of your skills and concern as the model itself.

Again regarding animation. This can be done in many ways to a greater or lesser degree, depending upon your amount of confidence, expertise, or just plain nerve, and range from a simple change of a leg or arm to the complete reworking of a basic kit. Whatever lengths you may wish to go to, major or minor, in so doing you will have infused a little of yourself and that is something good and creative in that you have expressed something of your sense of originality. Nonetheless, change or conversion should be to a purpose in that the subject should be doing something or involved in something. Much inspiration for this sort of thing in the Napoleonic field especially has sprung from the wealth of paintings and reproductions of them concerned with the overall period, and particularly Waterloo. There are available all manner of books and periodicals dealing with other equally colourful and interesting periods in which are to be found innumerable illustrations that can be interpreted as dioramas, or an interesting section can be picked out involving, say, a couple of figures or the selection of one particular horse and rider. I'm sure it's not necessary for me to carry on and describe exactly how or where inspiration can be brought about. You have your own bag and you'll know well enough where to go looking for ideas and when your fingers start twitching, something will have hit your eye.

However, another and perhaps more difficult approach is working strictly from scratch, knowing only that you want to do something which entails complete conversion of, perhaps, a horse and rider of your own special choice, posed in a way that you feel they should be. In these circumstances you have only your own imagination, a pile of assorted Historex parts, a clear-cut picture in your mind of how you want to manipulate these parts, tools, ingenuity and the enthusiasm for an original creation. All of that may sound pretty high minded but it is what you're basically up against. You'll have no nice clear painting or photograph in front of you to point up the position of a horse's leg or the way in which the rider sits the saddle from which you can technically transpose into three dimensional form, only either a fundamental understanding of human and equine anatomy or, failing this,

reference books on both to give you structural guidance and proportions. Another, possibly slightly easier, approach is to select a subject in a picture and then, using it for general detail reference, make it posed in the way you'd like it to be.

Naturally your personal level of confidence should indicate the direction to take and maybe the strength of your finances. Let's be perfectly honest. Although exceptional value, Historex parts and kits are not entirely cheap especially if you envisage a large diorama demanding extensive surgery. Therefore I'd strongly recommend that if you are planning to branch into the stimulating and satisfying realm of complete conversions starting with, say, a Montenegro Reservist of 1913 in all his colourful trappings, and your experience is very thin, shelve the idea and get into a simpler type, or have to hand all the information available, decide positively upon the pose and proceed very, very carefully. Indeed, the adage 'nothing ventured, nothing gained!' certainly applies, but also the cost of adventure and entering something of the untried is well worth a momentary thought.

For my own part I am first and foremost what might be best described as a general model maker and not essentially a military miniature specialist. My attitude is to make whatever appeals to me and that can amount to almost anything. But I do try to adhere to one firm rule which is, that whatever I attempt I investigate the original as deeply as I can, gathering as much information as is available because I find nothing is more disturbing than being in the dark about certain elusive details, especially when it comes to a scratch-built project.

My opinion is that Historex figures, horses and equipment are items unique in the realm of modelling, and notably the spare parts service. Little or no competition exists for them and their range of complete kits, admittedly of the Napoleonic era, is quite remarkable. Segom produce a pleasant product and their catalogue is far wider-ranging in types, but they tend to be a bit crude in a number of ways, albeit somewhat cheaper. Airfix have on the go their 'Collector's Series' which is proving to be a reasonable competitor, especially by way of price. However, at the time of writing, their output has been extremely limited and I'd say it's doubtful that they'll ever equal the Historex listings. It's a happy thought that what they do have are compatible in scale with Historex and can be interchanged should the need arise. Regrettably, the Airfix figures, mainly the equine ones, are irrevocably animated to the degree of uniform adornment following the 'pull' of material caused, for example, by a raised arm, and to change radically so tortuous a moulding can prove very difficult *if* you wish the soldier to remain of the same type. Problems are compounded by the fact that the torsos are in two halves, front and back, and hollow which means that a bit of fairly deep cutting can result in penetration of this shell. Any heat application to a hollow torso needs to be done with the greatest of care and attention otherwise considerable distortion can result. The characterization of Airfix faces is superb but unfortunately they come integral with the headgear, in two or three parts, incorporating the headwear, or, are flat-topped to take a hat. All of which doesn't entirely facilitate easy conversions.

On the credit side Airfix horses, with the possible exception of the gait of the Hussar's mount, their original issue, are very good in that they look sturdy and robust. Conversely, Historex hayburners tend towards being delicate, too narrow and with the appearance of thoroughbreds—which was often far from the truth in the case of military horses. Historex horses, you will note, have their legs, fore and aft per side, dead in line regardless of intended action from standing through to the gallop. Again, Airfix rider's legs are too bowed for my liking, leaving the impression that a horseman with legs like that when he sits around the house, *really* sits *around* the house. Furthermore, bones aren't shaped like that! But, as we've previously acknowledged, there is a price difference and I think that if Airfix set out to make figures in active postures, with accurate equipment details, selling at a nominal price to encourage the mildly interested and/or younger modellers, they've done a fantastic job.

Possibly a howl of protest will rise up when I say that, in my opinion, Historex figures are patently stiff and, by and large, characterless. Heads look straight ahead with unseeing eyes while necks are firmly moulded into squared-on collars. All torsos are of the same straight-backed form and vary only in decoration. Although standing and walking legs have a number of variations, riding legs are constant in form, altered only on the surface by the demands of the particular uniform. Obviously, from a manufacturing point of view, this is something of an ideal arrangement, much as in the motor industry you produce the same body shell and rearrange the chrome to get yourself a 'different' model and reduce the costs of retooling. But despite this criticism they are, 'out of the bag', exactly what I believe they're intended to be: individual, beautifully detailed miniature representations of given uniforms, to be assembled, lovingly painted and lined-up in some display facility in much the same manner as dummies are dressed and lined-up in museums. What I would dearly love to see in the Historex line is either the moulding of the collar to the torso—they do this very nicely for the worn pelisse— or the inclusion in the kits of a separate tunic collar in much the same way as they include gauntlets and cuffs. True, one can shave off the collar, position the head turned to either side, and fabricate a new collar cut from polystyrene card. Frequently though a particular collar will have on it a certain amount of lace which would be extremely hard to duplicate, aside from using paint, on the card. I can see no production problems here since all heads have a mould parting line running around them from side to side. Such a consideration, I feel, would help the less skilled to additional animation and would definitely add a further dimension to Historexcellence. An alternative, of course, is to gingerly sever the head at the top of the collar with an *exceptionally* fine-tooth saw and turn it to suit.

Another problem is endeavouring to rework a torso which bears a lot of intricate detailing across its front. If, for example, you wanted to animate a kit figure swivelling in the saddle with the shoulders at almost ninety degrees to the hips, you would be hard tried to duplicate the twist of the torso with the resulting, and essential for authenticity, pulling and creasing of the tunic 'fabric' and following distortion of braiding and so forth. Unless one were highly skilled with engraving tools or exceptionally capable in the manipulation of fine stretched sprue, such violent posturing would be tantamount to impossible. May I therefore throw in a suggestion that Historex tool for a number of their more complex torsos twisting to either side and, in so doing, elevate their already outstanding reputation even higher. Legs are simple enough to change, so are arms, but torsos are something else.

When I began animating Historex Napoleonic kits I did, in fact, do one soldier, a Cuirassier, twisting in the saddle as he brought back a high held sabre to make a slash. This action required that his shoulder line in section to that of his hips should be opposed at about forty-five degrees. To emphasize the movement he had to be leaning back from the waist which was taken care of by a wedge of plastic. The outcome I feel was successful, largely due to the fact that I selected a subject to which such a positive gesture could be made and which was helped by an unyielding breast and back plate. Another Napoleonic subject which I actively reanimated and which I knew would not give me a great amount of trouble was a Dutch Lancer standing in the stirrups, leaning forward from the waist and with his right arm fully extended ahead, hand gripping a lance parallel to the limb. His shoulders were opposed to the hips and I knew that it would be relatively simple to rectify a flat plastron were it necessary to do so. Therefore I think the lesson to be learned is that if you wish to effect a fairly violent body animation to a stock Historex figure, pick a subject with uncomplicated detail about the uniform which can be modified without loss of original authenticity.

As much as my brief for this book was to write about the converting of Historex figures, it would seem that my opinion is not entirely in their favour in view of several of the comments I've made so far. But don't you believe it! Historex to my mind is one of the best things to come along in years, and for the complete converter especially, their parts service. This service I feel is remarkable in the fullest sense of the word and is the best way I know for letting the imagination have its head and for turning up unlimited possibilities for foot and mounted figures, groups and dioramas. How many times have you

been intrigued by a particularly original piece only to learn that 'It's a Historex conversion'? In fact, that phrase is becoming part of the model-making fraternity's parlance. There is precious little in the whole gamut of military miniature ideas that cannot be accomplished through the aid of Historex parts combined with a degree of skill in the way of making a few items from scratch, the utilization of plastic card, plastic rod, the ability to stretch sprue, a modicum of craft knife dexterity and the aid of a good heat source in the form of either a Pyrogravure or miniature soldering iron. The fruits of one's endeavours are only limited by imagination and the determination to succeed in what you set out to do.

US Dragoon 1847

By way of passing on a measure of my experience in Historex converting, I selected as the mounted figure a relatively untapped area of the American forces of the past: a Dragoon Sergeant of the 1847 period. Surprisingly, research on the type was fairly difficult because there isn't exactly an abundance of information available. The American Civil and Indian Wars have been well documented and Hollywood, over several decades, has made certain that we know all about these eras. However, the Mexican War and the period of troubles with the Pawnee in which the Dragoons played a major part, along with General Zachary Taylor's columns, have had very little coverage. Indeed, there is not a vast difference between the uniform of the cavalry of those times and the American Civil War except that the waist-length tunic was of a tighter fitting type, though still of an indigo blue colour with yellow trim and NCO rank chevrons. In fact it was in 1847 that the US forces adopted the British style chevrons worn between the shoulder and elbow on either arm. Trousers were of the customary pale blue with yellow stripes for NCOs, while spurs and metal fittings were of brass, and belt, straps and carbine sling were white as distinct from the black leather adopted later. The significant difference was the high crowned, black leather peaked forage cap. Contrary to regulations a large number of cavalrymen took to wearing a yellow band for a touch of extra colour and distinction. My research sources were the *American*

Soldier series of illustrations painted by H. Charles McBarron, commissioned by the Chief of American Military History, Blandford's *Military Uniforms of the World*, written and illustrated by Preben Kannik, and a black and white wash sketch in the book *The Illustrations of Frederic Remington*. Saddlery information was gleaned from an article *The Development of the US Army Saddle*, by Stanley J. Olsen published in the *Military Collector & Historian* for spring 1955, furnished by my friend Cal Hurd of Washington DC. A touch of extra information was provided by Bob Percival from his extensive library pertaining to the early West.

I commence my figures by selecting what I think is a suitable Historex head and work on it to try and develop an expression befitting the general atmosphere that I wish to convey in the finished piece. In the case of the US Dragoon I saw it completed as a soldier in action, in a charge or melee, indicating a change of direction or pointing out something needing attention by those, since he was to be an NCO, under his command. I felt that such a gesture would not be made in a closed mouth manner which demanded that my first move was to effect an open-mouthed expression incorporating excitement and the shouting of an order. To do this I cut away the chin and the front of the jaw until the upper lip was reached and a definite orifice made. This done I built up another chin and lowered the jaw-

line with, as I wanted, the mouth open. Work around the aperture should be executed as cleanly as possible but the rest can be worked fairly roughly. When dried thoroughly the jaw can be smoothed off with a file and sand or emery paper. The filling substance used was Belco Cellulose Putty, obtainable at almost any car supply stores. A similar material is the American import commonly referred to as Green Stuff, although it is quite expensive for an average size tube. Cellulose putty can be bought in a can for a reasonable (at this writing) 33p for what must be about three times the quantity.

When attempting facial changes it's a good idea to stand in front of a mirror and make the desired expression on your own face and note what occurs muscularly to the features, then try to convey to the model head the things you've observed. To deepen or add lines, use the very point of your craft knife and draw it along sideways. Settle for the depth of score then round off the sides of the channel. Facial changes can be made by clipping the nose tip, notching the bridge of the nose, shaving the temples, hollowing the jaws and scoring furrows into the brow and between the eyebrows. Ears can be made by shaving flat one side of a length of plastic sprue of a gauge equal to the vertical distance

*Mouth opening. **A** Cleaned-up Historex head. **B** Cut back. **C** Mouth formed and new jaw. **D** Ledge for cap band.*

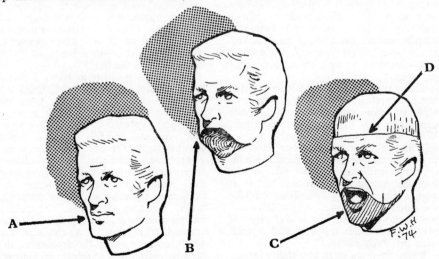

between the eye and the mouth and snipping off wedge shaped pieces towards the flattened side. These are cemented either side of the head and when perfectly dry can be further blended into the head and modelled.

Historex heads seem to lack the fullness of 'period' hair, even for Napoleonic times, especially at the back of the head. My Dragoon needed to have thick hair which partially covered the ears and was done in the following way. Originally I'd shaved off the mould seam-lines and removed the collar and added ears, so I now went around the brow and crown of the head with a pencil line approximately where the lower edge of his cap would sit. On this pencil line I cut a shallow incision and made a very narrow step on the upper side of it by shaving vertically all around. The step was of a depth to accommodate 20 thou plastic card from which the cap band would be cut.

From this gauge card I cut a 4mm ($\frac{6}{32}$") wide strip, long enough to go around the head. One end was placed on the ledge at the centre of the back of the head and tacked there with tube cement and then carried around the head, being secured with fluid cement as I went until coming back to the starting point. I cut off the excess material for a firm butt joint which was cemented to make the complete cylindrical form of the band.

With the glue set and firm, I used a dollop of cellulose putty to form the soft, somewhat bulbous top of the cap. Now came the treatment of the hair. I cut a thin strip of 20 thou plastic card of sufficient length to go roughly from one temple, around the back of the head and to the other temple, tooled it into a curve and cemented it into place below the cap edge.

Using the Pyrogravure with a pointed head, I carefully worked in a curly hair style on this extra piece, taking the precaution not to touch the cap band. With one of those indispensable mouse-tail files obtained from your Historex dealer Lynn Sangster, I filed a slight, narrow channel around the sides of the face and under the chin and laid in it a very thin strip of 5 thou plastic card for the chin strap. A moustache which completed the face, was just a tiny piece of plastic card under the nose and formed with the Pyrogravure.

I cemented the neck to a stalk of sprue and commenced painting the head. Doubtless the reader will have noticed that as yet I've made no mention of applying the peak of the cap. This has been omitted for a purpose. My main concern now was to paint the face and since it falls fairly close to the forehead it would tend to encumber the brush point in this area and around the eyes.

Painting, I believe, is something of a personal thing and amounts to every man to his own special techniques and choice of materials. However, deft painting can really infuse a lot of character and expression into the face which is otherwise difficult to accomplish through actual modelling in such small scale. Properly used colours can create a three-dimensional quality, in the way of wrinkles, ridges and so forth, on an otherwise flat surface. Tonal changes of flesh are seldom ever extreme and sharp and it is essential that one shade blends smoothly into another. The treatment of eyes should be handled in a subtle way thinking of them as *part* of the face and not overstating them with distinct black lines around the whites as if the figure concerned has been on a three week toot.

Take a look around you and observe the eyes of people and I think you will agree the whites of the eyes are really not that apparent. Lips should be of a tone only slightly redder than that of the overall basic face colour, and the same applies to cheeks, ears, nose and chin. Unless great care is taken with the 'colour modelling' of the face you will lose a human appearance and wind-up with that awful doll-like look which is frequently seen. With the face painted to my satisfaction I added the peak of the cap to finalize the part.

My next step was to go to work on the horse. Perhaps the reader will think it a little odd that I should dart from the man's head to the horse. However, I think the explanation is a fairly reasonable one and possibly worth thinking about when you're doing a similar thing. I see it not so much as a man *on* a horse, as man *and* horse whereby the rhythm of the horse's movement governs the posture of the rider and forms a flow of action between the two. Therefore, having established in my mind what the action is to be, worked on the head and set the atmosphere in the expression, the logical continuity is to select and animate horse parts which will contribute to the final concept of unity.

I'm fortunate in having a number of the various Historex horse parts and I went through them trying one to another for the most suitable combinations which, quite frankly, would also minimize the amount of chopping and changing I envisaged. This I think is always a good thing to remember since I can't see the point of inflicting upon oneself any more work than is necessary to arrive at a given stance or gait. After much deliberation I finally settled for right side No 6 and for the left side, the front half of No 11 and half of No 7 for the rear. My horse needed to be travelling at a full gallop which I think is quite a hard thing to accomplish convincingly. The ideal of

course is to have all four hooves almost touching under the body and the animal completely off the ground, which of course is one phase of the galloping cycle. Try as I may I've not been able, outside of using sky hooks, to come up with a means of creating such a moment in any of my galloping horses.

I think perhaps the closest I did come to it was by drilling up into the rear leg closest to the ground, then drilling through the centre of a length of clear plastic sprue, running a thin piece of steel piano wire through it and into the leg and cementing the end of the sprue

Relocation of horse legs. **A** *Vertical cut.* **B** *Saw.* **C** *Saw cut.* **D** *Lengthwise posterior cut.* **E** *Cut out of body for fit.* **F** *Fill.*

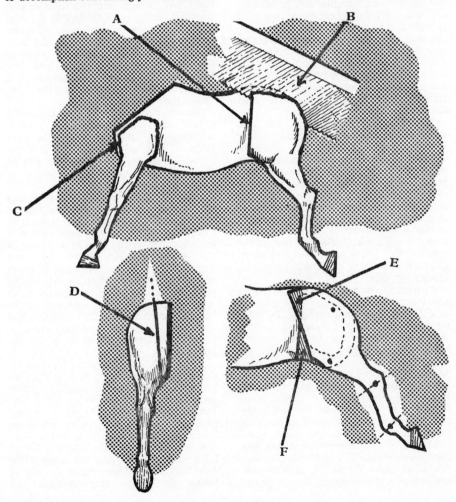

to the hoof. The other end of the wire was in turn sunk into the base and a *quick* glance did give the impression that all four hooves were off the ground. But closer study made it clear just what was going on and the conviction of it was lost. As it so happens I went on to complete horse and rider and resolved the clear sprue problem by having the horse in high 'grass'. Of course you could probably do it by having the horse's belly resting on a convenient tree stump or on a remarkably high tuft of grass made up of a number of 30 thou card blades . . . but I think that's enough of that idea.

All horse leg changes should be made before the two halves are finally cemented together allowing for full accessibility to the limbs being doctored and permitting any *inside* reinforcement or filling. If it is intended to make a change involving the shoulder or hip, remove the leg completely by cutting on the outer side diagonally, immediately in front of the stifle to about half way through, then making another saw cut from the posterior, right through the rump to meet up with the first cut.

With the entire leg free you can swivel it against the body section where it came from until you find the new location that you want. Depending upon whether the leg is to go forward or back you'll find it necessary to trim away parts of it or parts of the body at the edge of the cut to make it adopt a natural relationship. In the process of such major changes as this it is imperative that you remain mindful of the horse's skeleton and where exactly the joints are. Reference to Chapter 11 of this book will keep you straight on this.

As with the human, so with the horse, any given movement motivates a series of changes, slight and extreme, of bone structure, muscles and ligaments which, if your modifications are to be successful, must be considered and worked to. To help with this a good idea is to mark with a large pencil dot where the joint is located before cutting and cut *through* it. The dot should be large enough to be seen half on either side when the leg sections are separated which means that you'll have a 'key' as you figure new positions. To whichever direction the joint is to swivel, 'V' either side from the dot axis, out. To arrive at the new position you will, in effect, bring together

and cement both sides of the 'V'. Having made this change there'll be a gap on the opposite side which can be easily filled with cellulose putty, body putty or molten sprue on the Pyrogravure and reformed using the yet undisturbed leg as a guide. Often the pasterns, the bones connecting the fetlock joints to the coronets or upper part of the hooves, are too thick in a lot of the mouldings and need to be thinned down by shaving for a more delicate appearance.

Having made your leg changes, try the two complete halves together and check for a natural relationship between all four limbs. As much as a horse's legs pass through a cycle of movements in the course of the gallop or any other gait, the follow-through as such is that the right fore is back and the right rear is forward, while the left fore is forward and the left rear is backward. This you will appreciate is extreme simplification but for a natural look the legs should be related so. Before tying-up the body and limb halves for the complete animal there are a couple of other things which you might think about.

The first of these is best described by saying that when you, as a human, standing up, take the weight of your body off one leg you'll notice that the leg *taking* the weight causes that side of the hip to push up, off the horizontal. It happens also as you walk.

So it is with the horse. If one of its legs is on the ground momentarily taking the weight it stands to reason that there'll be a slight raising of the load bearing side of the rump or, in the case of a foreleg, a rise in the shoulder. If you have the opportunity, watch a horse as it walks and you'll see this weight change taking place in the rump and the shoulders. It is most apparent in the walk but as the horse increases its speed through trot and canter to gallop, the increased momentum of the legs tends to even out the body.

You could, understandably, dismiss this suggestion as being relatively unimportant and argue that nobody notices such a thing when a horse is moving fast. But remember also that you as the modeller and, if I may say so, artist, are 'freezing' a moment in time. So the point is that when you bring the body halves together finally, having the ground leg side fractionally higher than the other, filling the slight step created and smoothing across would not be out of place.

Secondly there's the little matter of the horse's width. Historex horses are too narrow and require shimming between the halves to impart a bit more heft to their appearance. An increase of 1½mm ($\frac{1}{16}$") is what I allow in the hindquarters and a piece fractionally thinner between the shoulders. You can if you wish stick a length of $\frac{1}{16}$" (60 thou) plastic card the length of the horse's body on one side and almost the depth from back to chest, trim it to outline and then, laying it flat side down on an equally flat piece of wet and dry emery, carefully sand down until have have a wedge shape on the addition by bearing down more at the shoulder end. This done, the halves can be cemented together. When perfectly dry I suggest you shave out the posterior to balance the one sided thickness which the shim has caused.

With work completed on the horse's body the next logical move is the attachment of neck and head. A couple of methods which I employ may well be worth passing on. Start either one by severing the head from the neck immediately behind the jaw bone and describing a line as close as you can up to the poll, which is the point of the head between the ears.

Assuming that the moulded neck is a straight one, carefully make a vertical cut with a saw through the *length* of it centrally from top to bottom to wind up with two halves. With a strip of plastic card make a shim at the shoulder end of the neck sufficient to equal the width of the widened shoulders and attach it to *one* side.

If you wish to have the neck turning or twisting, immerse both halves in actively boiling water and let them swim around in the bubbles for a spell until you think they've had long enough to soften them. With a cloth handy to protect your delicate fingers, fish out a half with tweezers and quickly, using the cloth, bend or twist the piece as you want it laterally. Do the same with the other half, endeavouring to duplicate the shape of the previous piece so that when the two halves are together they should pretty well match.

The idea of this is to avoid what so often occurs when you try to make neck changes with heat and a solid lump of plastic: you deform and distort a lot of that nice muscle moulding which is difficult to re-establish. Furthermore, two halves are much thinner than a lump and are more easily influenced by the heat of the water.

When you've got your shaping right, cement the two halves together with the shim piece between the neck ends and nothing at the head end, fill where necessary and smooth off. If you find one side to be slightly longer than the other at the head end, trim off as required. Now try the head to the neck and work it around for a pleasing relationship with the neck and in keeping with the movement you've effected. When satisfied, cement it in place with tube cement and again, fill and smooth as necessary. The neck can now be fixed to the shoulders.

The other method for neck changes is to dispose of the moulded neck after removing the head but keeping it handy for future muscle reference. Cut from the 60 thou plastic card a neck outline and warm it over the flame of, preferably, a meths burner for cleanliness. If you haven't one of these then a candle will supply the heat but a bit of soot with it.

When the plastic shows signs of flopping, again with the aid of a cloth, twist or bend it into a desired shape and let it cool. Tentatively, with tube cement, attach the head to that end of the plastic and try it against the shoulders of the body and move it around until your judgment tells you that, in silhouette, both flow into the body and balance is correct and do the final cementing at both shoulders and head end.

When dried firmly, fill out the roundness of the neck either side of the cut-out with Brummer stopping or cellulose putty. Both substances being applied reasonably thick will, in their curing process, develop a skin on the surface while the material below will continue to remain pliable for a time.

Now, using a pointed but rounded—anything other than sharp—wooden modelling tool, or the point of a brush for Brummer's, gently work in the muscle structure with curving indentations which will, in my experience, turn out far more pleasing a result than trying to carve into a build-up of blobbed-on molten plastic, body putty or something similar.

When done this neck area should be

given at least overnight to thoroughly set and dry out. With all of these things done you should go around the horse filling and smoothing where necessary, using 400 wet and dry to finish off.

A word of caution. If you've filled and modelled the neck with Brummer stopping, keep the wet emery away from it. Instead, dry sand and then seal with a couple of coats of shellack or button polish.

On the Dragoon's horse, after it was satisfactory as a model creature, I did not lash paint but went ahead and started building on the saddlery. For the saddle blanket I used folded and plastic-saturated (a mixture of tube cement and chloroform) tissue paper well pressed onto the back so that it would 'sit' with the minimum of bulk.

With the plastic solution not fully set and the blanket still mildly yielding, I calculated where the straps of the martin-dale would pass over the front of the blanket to join the saddle and impressed the tissue at those positions. Thus, when the straps were eventually attached, they would give the impression of flattening the material.

The US Army cavalry saddle of that time was the 1841 pattern Grimsley which was not unlike a British style saddle with its long leather skirts to protect the rider's legs. It had a high pommel and a slightly higher, spooned cantle, both of which were mortised to take straps for the cloak in front and cylindrical valise at the back. It had a quilted seat sown and stitched crosswise and the sidebars, or numnahs, had iron rings and staples for the attachment of the valise, shoe pouch, crupper, water bottle and oats bag, if carried.

The stirrups were of Dragoon pattern and made of brass and the leathers buckled over the arches.

With my horseman depicted as 'out' of the saddle it was necessary that I completed all these parts in some measure of detail. However, if a rider is posed 'sitting' the saddle it can oftentimes impart a stronger feeling of a good 'seat' if only pommel and cantle are cemented to the rider before his attachment to the horse to eliminate the possibility of a too high look. I think this especially applies in the case of scratch-building.

I moulded the saddle, made the valise, shoe pouch and so forth, and cut the skirts from 20 thou plastic card. But before placing and cementing these I installed the girth and then put the skirts over it. According to the McBarron painting the cloak was housed in a sleeve of the same colour as the rider's trousers, with what would appear to be a rawhide leather insert to prevent saddle rub. This sleeve extends from one side of the pommel at, say, the level of the rider's left knee and over to his right knee height. I made the cloak sleeve by rolling up a length of tissue, saturating it with plastic solution as I went until I reached the approximate scale bulk of the item, and secured the roll for permanency.

I think you would find it useful to know that when I commenced the roll I implanted a length of thin copper wire so that when finished and ready to be fitted to the pommel, it would remain in whatever position was required. This should be a useful pointer to keep in mind with any form of such roll which needs to be bent around something. It avoids that pesky problem of having to fight the thing into place and hold it until the glue sets.

With the saddlery done I turned my attention to fitting the rider's legs for correct positioning and 'hang'. I used Dragoon legs because of their pantaloon style and suitable spurs. I straightened them by applying the Pyrogravure to the back of the knees and dropped the boot toes by heat cutting into the front of the ankles.

As I progressed I continually tried the still separated legs to the saddle until I got the position I wanted, which entailed a little shimming between the hips. I next melted scrap sprue around the seat and front of the trousers to fill the gaps and built up and out at the rear of the waist and compensated this by cutting in at the front which, in effect, brought the angle of the hips more in line with the upper legs.

The torso was treated in a similar way in that the left shoulder dropped and the right one came forward. I built out the front of the right shoulder and side of the chest and shaved off across the rear of the shoulder and shoulder blade, cleaned it up and did the same thing in reverse on the opposite shoulder. Cemented to the hips and turned slightly to the left, I attained the desired feeling of the man turning at an approxi-mate forty-five degree angle to the hips in a natural manner rather than looking

Right *As perhaps a fallen Mexican may have seen a US Dragoon (as modelled by Bill Hearne in Chapter 3) at Buena Vista. A low perspective shot of the figure points up the sought-after cohesion of man and horse. A line flow between the two is essential in such an equestrian subject to create a convincing feeling of movement.*
Below *Both mane and tail of the horse were made from nylon string, combed out, dyed black and fused with the help of a Pyrogravure. These were attached, after the horse was painted, with the excellent Permabond cement.*

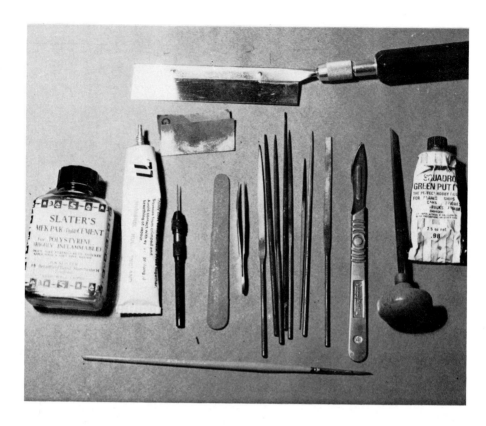

Above *A selection of plastic figure modeller's tools, chosen by Sid Horton. Included are a razor saw, sandpaper, liquid and tube cement, Squadron Green Putty, pin drill, emery board, tweezers, collection of fine files, craft knife, gouge and paintbrush.* **Below** *The two figure conversions described by Roy Dilley in Chapter 2, shown here in their unpainted state to illustrate the different materials used in their construction.*

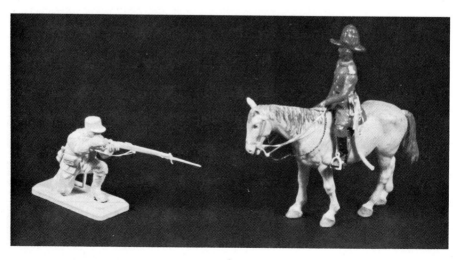

Above left *Grenadier of the 3rd Foot (The Buffs) 1725, converted basically from the SEGOM 18th Century Artilleryman by 'Mac' Kennaugh. Modifications include new coat turnbacks and hat from plastic card.* **Above right** *Cornet of the 2nd Horse (The Queen's Bays) 1685, another SEGOM conversion by 'Mac' Kennaugh. Basic figure is the drummer of the Mousquetaires du Roi, which involves filing down the basic torso to accept a Historex cuirass and considerable work on the legs to enable the figure to sit a Historex horse.* **Below** *some of Joe Gadd's large scale Airfix conversions. From left to right they are a trooper of the 21st Empress of India's Lancers 1914; Coldstream Guards drummer; officer, 11th Prince of Wales' Own Lancers 1914; gunner, Royal Garrison Artillery 1914; basic Airfix Household Cavalry figure; trooper, Queen's Bays 1900; officer, 1st Duke of York's Own Lancers; staff sergeant, Royal Scots Greys 1914; and officer, Coldstream Guards.*

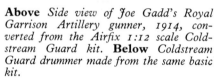

Above *Side view of Joe Gadd's Royal Garrison Artillery gunner, 1914, converted from the Airfix 1:12 scale Coldstream Guard kit.* **Below** *Coldstream Guard drummer made from the same basic kit.*

Above *Front view of the Royal Garrison Artillery gunner whose construction is described in Chapter 5.* **Below** *Joe Gadd's conversion of the Airfix Lifeguard Trumpeter to a Royal Scots Greys Staff Sergeant, 1914.*

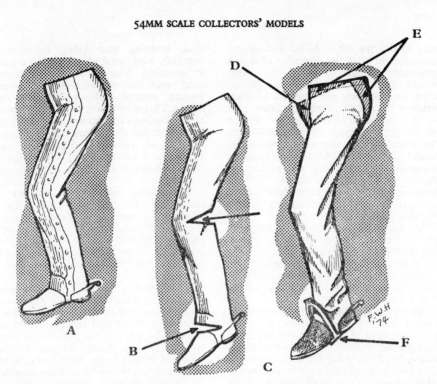

Straightening legs. **A** *Historex riding leg.* **B** *Cut and bend foot down; fill.* **C** *Cut and open; fill.* **D** *Cut away.* **E** *Fill and remodel.* **F** *Attach stirrups to completed leg.*

as if there was some sort of roller bearing located between hips and torso. Some further adjustment was made to the shoulders by raising the right one for his raised sword arm and lowering the left.

Perhaps the reader's feelings are the same as my own when it comes to seeing hands that do not *grip* sword handles and reins, and it's unfortunate that an otherwise excellent piece of work should be marred by this, almost built-in, problem of model soldiers. The answer however is, if you'll pardon the pun, at hand. Lynn Sangster, through his parts service, can provide drummer's arms which have hands gripping sticks and things. These are basically similar to the general range of Historex arms and can be re-animated or used as they are.

I think the tendency seems to be to assemble a figure and then add, say, a sword with the hand and arm linked to the rest of the body. I personally prefer to fix the sword or whatever to the hand *before* it is combined with the figure as a

whole. This way allows you to poise the hand in relationship to the overall posture and permits an easier working situation; not to mention the fact that if you don't like how things turn out, you'll not have to worry about anything beyond rectifying the arm and sword unit.

My Dragoon's sword hand was drilled into, an extension spigot from the sword blade was let into the hole, I made a pommel to emerge from the rear of the clenched palm, and finally a guard was fabricated in stretched sprue to encase the hand. This to my mind would seem to be a logical series of steps for a convincing result and in consideration of the 1:30 scale of the completed figure.

French pilot 1914-18

My second conversion is a foot figure representing a pilot of the French Air Service in the course of the 1914-1918 War. I think perhaps this particular character has a couple of things going for him which are worth drawing to your attention. Firstly, there's the posture of leaning against something with one foot crossed over the other, and second the 'leather' flying coat which he wears.

The French Air Service during the Great War functioned in much the same

C

way as did the other Allied and enemy countries in that the majority of flying personnel transferred from other regiments and units and, in so doing, continued to wear the uniform of their original branch. Towards the latter part of the war uniforms indigenous to the air services emerged, as for example the 'buttoned across the chest' maternity jacket of the RFC/RAF and the French-adopted horizon blue, single-breasted tunics with up-and-down collars, breeches with thin, twin red stripes down the sides, brown leather gaiters or blue puttees and boots.

My figure I felt needed to transmit an air of nonchalance, having perhaps survived yet another day of aerial combat over the Front, as he leans against his aircraft with his kepi stuffed under one arm, the hand of which is in turn sunk into a pocket.

To a suitable Historex head I gave the mould line shaving treatment, trimmed the hair, gave it ears and removed the Napoleonic collar. This I went ahead and painted, working for the expression that I felt it should have and which would duly influence the overall attitude of the completed subject.

My next step was to go ahead and try for the leg position. I say 'try' because one is never really certain about pulling off an entirely new stance. The results of my efforts can be seen in the photographs. The anatomical considerations were as follows. Because the body weight is being taken on the left leg, that side of the hip is pushed up, while the other side drops and accordingly lowers the height of the knee of the right leg. Meanwhile, the right arm is helping maintain balance resting upon something, which causes the right shoulder to raise slightly while the other shoulder slopes down into what is a relaxed left arm.

It is not overly important which pair of *standing* Historex legs you use for such a figure position as this provided they lend themselves to modification of the costume. This pose, to some extent, is a useful one in that it could be applied to a horse soldier standing alongside his mount with his arm resting on the saddle seat, chatting-up a couple of birds. Such a print is to be seen in the book *European Military Uniforms* by Paul Martin, and could be turned into a fascinating three-dimensional vignette.

This animation calls for little more

than wedging and filling to change normally horizontal planes, when a man is standing four-square, to converse ones, and the consideration of maintaining natural balance through the figure. This of course is all part and parcel of the business of anatomy and it's to be recommended that if you have a sincere interest in advanced converting you should have a rudimentary knowledge of bone structure of both animals and humans.

So, getting back to the subject in hand. With the legs completed, I fixed them at the waist to the torso and fused the two with additional molten plastic on the Pyrogravure and added the head. This now began to indicate that I was going the right way for the stance that I wanted.

The breeches were built-up by roughly cutting the wing shapes for the outer thighs from 60 thou plastic card, tacking them in position and fusing them with the legs by melting the plastic. Satisfied with the general shape I went ahead and filed and sanded in the folds and creases.

Drapery of course is another area for study and is very important to the finished model. So how 'clothing' twists, pulls and wrinkles with body movement, and the manner in which creases and folds radiate from shoulders, elbows, knees, belts and equipment carried, is something else you'd do well to thoroughly investigate if you want your modelling to be fully convincing.

Because the tunic of my airman was only exposed at the front, I was able to lay on the right side of the skirt and blend it into the waist, indenting slightly where the bottom button pulled the 'material'. From the same 10 thou plastic card I cut the complete left side of the tunic front from the shoulder to the hem of the skirt and placed it on the figure for an obvious edging where the sides met and overlapped. While the plastic was still yielding after cementing I pressed in, with a small modelling tool, slight button hollows and a bit of 'pull' on the skirt at the lowest button position. Only when this area was completely dry did I drill into the five button positions and insert the spigots of rolled-back plastic rod for the buttons themselves. The tunic collar was attached as were the breast and side pockets.

To make the 'leather' flying coat I used a smooth type of tissue paper.

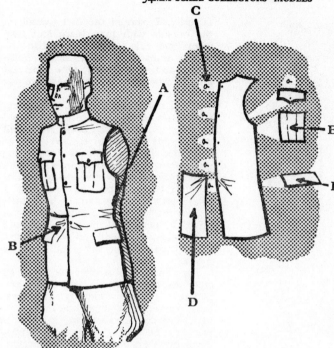

Method for making fly-front tunic. **A** Tunic flap and skirt blended to torso. **B** Skirt of tunic blended to torso. **C** Buttons. **D** Right skirt. **E** Breast pocket. **F** Side pocket flap.

Usually, if tissue is to be used, it's a good idea to wrinkle and ball it up and roll it between the palms of the hands to break down the fibres and make it more pliable. For this job, wanting a fairly smooth finish, I cut and worked the paper as it was.

To make a coat like this one has literally got to tailor it to fit the figure. The parts comprise: two fronts combining the lapels, one full back piece and the collar, while the heavy sleeves are made up out of suitable gauge scrap sprue. Although the front of the coat is flopping open, the front pieces must be cut in consideration of it being fully buttoned up across the chest. The front pieces were also required to drape from the shoulders and this was done by laying the parts on a fairly thick magazine and impressing them *lengthwise*, commencing lightly just below the shoulders and getting broader and heavier down towards the hems.

Depicting substantial leather I aimed more for rolls than tight creases. The lapels were folded and rolled into the fronts for further effect. and were misshapen a little as an indication of wear and tear. As I went along I periodically tried the parts to the figure for certainty

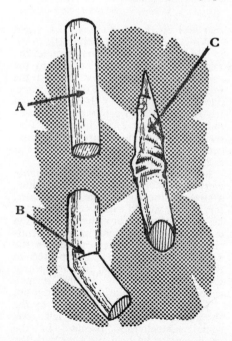

Arms made from scrap sprue. **A** *round scrap sprue.* **B** *cut and bent.* **C** *cut to fit shoulder and side of torso.*

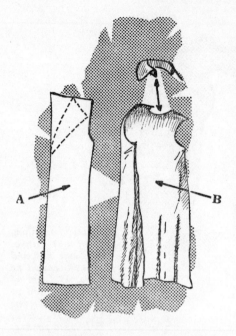

Flying coat cut-outs. A coat front, cut out two sides. B coat back curved and creased.

that they fitted and the 'hang' was right.

When completed I cemented the fronts in place on the shoulders, around the arm holes and down a little from the armpits after having *first* painted the uniform and the *insides* of the coat fronts. The back of the coat falls directly from the shoulders with a few minor creases radiating from the lower arm holes. This was fitted to the figure's back and cemented across the shoulders and around the arm holes.

My tailoring calculations having worked out correctly, the joining points, a straight line down from the armpits, met as they should with a very slim overlap which allowed for cementing and the completion of the coat body. A semicircular piece of paper was cut for the collar, folded, fitted and cemented to tie up with the lapels, and the whole thing was treated on the outside to a coating of plastic solution to stiffen it up.

When dry I fitted the arms to the shoulders. One of these, the left, took some manoeuvring because in the crook was to be held the kepi with the hand in the pocket. I brought it about by a little filing here and there on the hat and arm until the two combined satis-

factorily. I painted the coat overall on the outside with matt black and then went over this with black indian ink which imparts a soft, shiny finish similar to that of leather. One hand and a scarf were provided and the figure was complete.

I will not involve myself in painting techniques since this subject is covered by other authors in the book. But I will draw your attention to the use of Tempera Powder colours for toning generally over painted surfaces but particularly for a really convincing look of dust on boots, knees and backsides. I used it on the Dragoon and on his horse's hooves and legs and I also used it on the aviator's boots. Soldiers in the field tend to get dusty and dirty and powder paint is ideal for bringing this about on your models.

I acknowledge that there may be many who do not entirely agree with my particular methods and/or techniques, but doubtless they are among those who have had considerable experience with Historex converting and, accordingly, developed ways and means of their own. But those I've tried to pass on have served me well and I can only hope that they will prove of some value to those less familiar with modelling but anxious to improve.

Airfix conversion— SS cavalry trooper

After my series of articles on the Light Brigade in *Airfix Magazine* I thought it would be interesting to try a completely different period, so I attempted an SS cavalry trooper for this book. I now think it possible to turn almost anything into anything else you want, with a little thought and varying degrees of hard work. Hard work, he says. Well, I enjoy it. Most of my reference material finishes at 1900 so I'm afraid what little I have been able to glean on the SS cavalry is scanty to say the least, but what little I have is contained below.

One good source of information on the SS is a series of books, *Uniforms of the SS*, Volume 6, by Andrew Mollo, being particularly useful, containing as it does, a wealth of material on uniforms, equipment, rank badges and insignia, etc.

8th SS Kavallerie Division 'Florian Geyer' was formed in September 1942 by expanding the existing SS Cavalry

Brigade (1st and 2nd Florian Geyer SS Cavalry Regiments, plus SS recce and artillery detachments). The division served in the Balkans and Hungary, and included the 15th, 16th, 17th and 18th SS Cavalry Regiments besides the normal ancillary units. It was in Hungary in April 1944 for Operation Margarethe and with XII SS Cavalry Division (Maria Theresa) formed the IX SS Korps. It was one of the nine divisions left in Budapest when the Russians advanced that December. These divisions fought on to the very end, Pest being taken in January and Buda on 13th February, after bitter house-to-house fighting. Thousands of men from the division were captured and with the fall of Budapest, the division officially and physically ceased to exist.

Collar patches were SS runes. Cuff title 'Florian Geyer' from 1944. According to *Divisions of the Waffen SS* (Beadle & Hartmann, Key Publications) the Florian Geyer earlier regiments were in Russia in the summer of 1941 and the Divisional Commander 1940-2 and 1943-4 was Hermann Fegelein.

The basis of this conversion are the Airfix kits of the Hussar and the 'Scots Grey', but you will also need the rifle, water bottle, gas mask case, canteen, spade, binoculars, bread bag and cap insignia from the Armour Accessories range marketed by Lynn Sangster (see appendix). I will not deal with the techniques of conversion, except where they become necessary, as these are explained elsewhere in this book.

The tools I have used are shown in one of the photographs but you may have your own personal preferences. They are, for the most part, self-explanatory, but perhaps some need a little explanation. The razor saw at the top of the photograph is used for heavy cutting, such as removing the legs from the horse, etc. The liquid cement, in this case Mek-Pak, is used to cement all the small pieces, because it is more controllable than tube cement. It is applied with a brush and if there is any residue all you have to do is to blow over the surface. This evaporates the cement before it can mark the surface. The pin-vice holding a needle is used to apply small amounts of Green Stuff and to work it up into the hairlike texture of the hair and the mane of the horse. The emery board, files and scalpel are self-

explanatory. The engraving tool is used to work on the 'hair' after the Green Stuff has dried, for a finer texture than can be achieved with a needle in the pin vice alone. Lastly, the 'Green Stuff', or, more correctly, Squadron Green Putty, a filler I have found no alternative for. It dries hard, does not crumble or flake away when carved or sanded to shape and can be used in quite large amounts, without any fear of it dripping off the finished figure.

Take the horse halves from the Hussar kit, cement together and allow to dry out overnight. While this is happening, you can proceed with the rest of this conversion. I will come back to the horse later.

Head take the head from the Hussar kit and carefully, using a razor saw, remove about the top third of the busby. Then, with a new blade in the scalpel, carve the basic shape of the field cap. Carefully carve away the moustache and shape the upper lip. The cheeks can also be hollowed out at this point and the 'bruiser' type nose fined down by carefully paring away the sides. This should completely change the character of the face. Sand as smooth as possible, using a scrap of fine wet and dry. Then wash Mek-Pak over the whole face and cap with a brush. Leave for a few seconds and then blow on it to evaporate the cement. This should melt away any sharp edges left from the carving.

Using a razor saw, saw straight and level into the front of the face on a level with the base of the cap to take a peak made from the plastic card supplied in these kits. Cement the peak in place and build up the hair from the Green Stuff, applied in small amounts with the needle and worked up into a hairlike texture. Now cut a 'V' from the front of the collar so that it looks as if it has been left open, and sand smooth. The cap insignia from Armour Accessories can be cemented in place with Mek-Pak and, in my case, a cigarette added from stretched sprue. Remove most of the sprue below the collar. Place the head on one side.

Body and arms use the body from the 'Grey kit. Carefully carve all decoration from the body halves and sand smooth. Remove the coatee tails with a razor saw and cement the body halves together. Allow to dry. When thoroughly dry saw away the raised collar and enlarge the hole at the neck to take the stub beneath the head. Cement the head in place and either build up the collar with Green Stuff or make a completely new collar out of plastic card. Cement this in place with Mek-Pak or a similar liquid adhesive. Take the arms from the Hussar kit, carve away all the decoration and carve the cuffs to the new shape of elasticated cuffs. Very little else needs to be done to them but I have cut the hands away at the wrist and cemented them into their new positions. This has to be done by trial and error to find a position to suit your figure, or whim. Now cement the arms to the body. The smock can now be built up, using liberal amounts of Green Stuff and remembering that the smock was a very loose fitting garment. The easiest way of doing this is to apply the Green Stuff with an old knife blade. As it dries a skin forms on its surface and this can be moulded with the fingers. As you do so, folds will form. The waist of the smock can be drawn in by cutting a piece of notepaper slightly smaller than the width of the belt and, pulling it tight around the waist of the figure, the Green Stuff will now have convincing folds in it. Remove any surplus. When dry a belt of plastic card can be cemented in place. The smock may need sanding smooth and the joints between arms and body filled and sanded smooth. The 'Y' straps can be added from plastic card, but all other detailing left until the figure is finished.

Legs take the legs from the Hussar kit. Carve away the raised stripe down both sides and remove the mould lines, sand smooth, then using a sharp blade, cut into the legs just below the knee. This will form the top of the boots. Carve the boots to shape. When satisfied with the basic shape sand smooth. Then, using a fine rat tailed file, the folds round the ankles can be made. Carve the riding breeches into the knee, remembering that they tuck into the boots. The legs are now cemented together. Small pieces of scrap sprue are cemented to the backs of the thighs. These will form the basis of the fullness of the riding breeches. When the cement is completely dry, cover the sprue with Green Stuff and shape using the fingers. Sand smooth. Cement the legs to the figure. The bottom of the smock is built up with Green Stuff using the same technique as for the top. When thoroughly

dry, sand smooth.

I find it easiest to paint the figure at this point, before any of the equipment is cemented in place, because of the complicated pattern of the smock. Also, some of the equipment has to hang over the horse, or the equipment on the horse. Painting details, colours, etc, are at the end of this chapter.

Horse take the horse which you have already cemented together and carefully, with a razor saw, and using a 45 degree cut, remove the front offside leg, complete with all its intended muscles. When you have done this, saw right through this leg twice, at the knee and at the hock. Remove a small triangular piece of plastic from the inside hock and cement the hoof onto the leg, as in the drawings. Now add a small wedge of plastic inside the knee, and cement the two parts of the leg together. You should now have a straight leg. This, in turn, is cemented back onto the horse and any slight, or not so slight, gaps are filled. The whole thing is allowed to dry out thoroughly.

The rest of the horse can be left as it is or, as I have done, remove a wedge of plastic from the neck before the head is cemented in place, so that the head tilts forward. As regards the mane, a flying mane on a standing horse looks a little incongruous, to say the least. The mane can be built up from body putty, worked up into a hairlike texture. The forelock is from the Hussar kit. The tail, I'm afraid, I cheated on and took from the Airfix Polish Lancer.

Horse blanket, saddle flaps and the saddle itself come from the 'Grey kit. Little has to be done to them at all, but you can fill the area between the saddle and its flaps, after it has been cemented in place. The saddle bags over the horse's shoulders are made from laminated

Key to drawings. 1 Hussar head as per kit. 2 Hussar head, remove shaded area. 3 the basic shape you should have left. 4 the finished head. 5 basic 'Grey body. 6 remove shaded areas. 7 basic body shape. 8 the finished half of the upper body, black areas are filling. 9 Hussar legs. 10 the cuts required. 11 basic shape showing added sprue. 12 the finished legs, black area filling again. 13 the finished figure minus arms. 14 the basic Hussar arm. 15 showing the cuts. 16 black areas are filling. 17 the finished arm. Note also detail sketches of arm, cap and collar insignia.

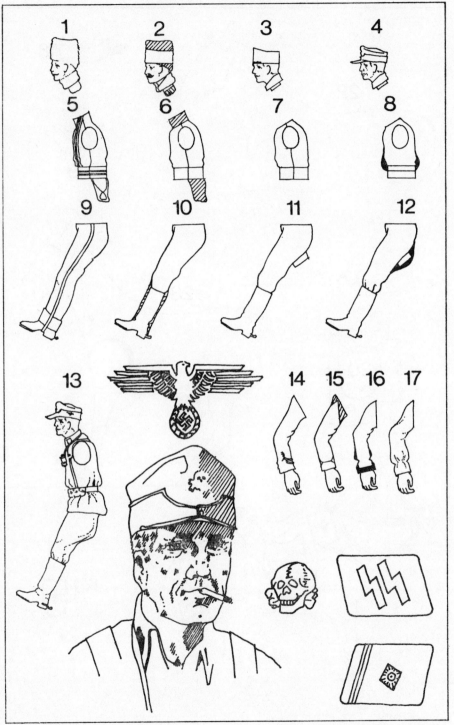

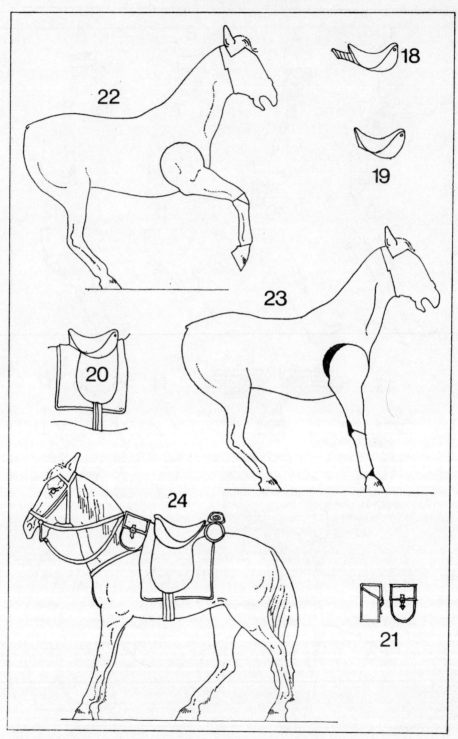

plastic card. The drawings are actual size. The spade and mess tin from Armour Accessories; the camouflaged helmet is a Tamiya one from the spares box.

You are now ready for the part of the work I enjoy most but which tends to frighten off a lot of people, and prevent them taking an interest in figure modelling. I've only one tip here, and that is, keep it simple. But I make no apologies for not giving any tips on the techniques of painting for I am sure each of you have your own, so I will only give the colours here: field cap—field grey, dull silver insignia (silver-grey) toned with black; jacket collar—either black or later field grey. Pale grey insignia on black squares (avoid white or silver because they are far too bright, and an overall

muted appearance is best); smock—see camouflage drawing for notes; rank insignia—emerald green on black silk; riding breeches—field grey; boots—black (again, avoid black, shade with greys); spurs—steel; water bottle, gas mask case—field grey; bread bag—paler field grey; spade—field grey, wooden handle; all leather work on the horse is dark brown, although the saddle bags could be lighter; horse blanket—dark neutral grey, almost black. Avoid all startling colours, such as silver, black or white—use greys for these. All the detailing to the figure can now be done, and all the equipment painted and cemented in place.

I hope you will enjoy this conversion and that it may give you ideas of your own.

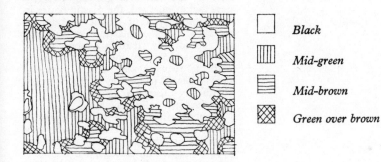

☐ Black

▥ Mid-green

☰ Mid-brown

▨ Green over brown

Key to drawings. **18** *basic 'Grey saddle, remove shaded area.* **19** *finished saddle.* **20** *finished saddle, basic assembly.* **21** *saddle bags. Make two of these (side and front elevation shown.)* **22** *offside of Hussar horse showing cuts.* **23** *Hussar horse showing the new position of the leg.* **24** *finished horse.*

four

'Mac' Kennaugh
Acetate figures

One form of plastic which has not received a great deal of attention, although it has tremendous possibilities, is the form of acetate used in the products of another French company, SEGOM. In this chapter 'Mac' Kennaugh, a well-known modeller, contributor to various modelling magazines and a former editor of IPMS Magazine, describes some of the possibilities of these kits and a few simple conversion projects.

For a good many years figures of model soldiers, with a few exceptions, were restricted to cast metal 'toys' or limited production types for collectors, and though there were a number of dedicated enthusiasts it is perhaps understandable that the hobby appeal was somewhat restricted. Coincidentally with the sudden expansion of types available to what is now a vast and ever growing range, a new factor emerged, the plastic figure in 'workable' types of plastic. I refer to workable types of plastic because if we are completely truthful there is no entirely satisfactory method of working with the 'rubbery' soft plastics, as one of their inherent properties is that they are chemically inert and unaffected by adhesives generally available.

The principal pioneer with this new medium was of course Historex, who took advantage of the potential of plastics to produce superb mouldings, which modellers experienced in plastic modelling soon started 'converting' with great effect. Airfix have followed suit and have an ever increasing range of first class quality, but there is also a third range of products which is not generally well known though they have been available for some time. I refer to the plastic kits produced by SEGOM in France, which are now readily available from Model Figures & Hobbies, Belfast, and Seagull Models, London.

SEGOM are different, very different, because they are moulded in an acetate plastic which requires acetone as an adhesive, and also because the kits include a small packet of 'bits' which can be dissolved in acetone and used thinned as glue or thick as a filler.

Acetate requires a different technique in handling, and where you would use a combination of knife/file/sandpaper on polystyrene, a very sharp knife is all you really need with acetate. I must confess when I first tipped the contents of a SEGOM kit on my modelling table I was not over-impressed, but close inspection revealed very well moulded detail. However, it was some months before I got down to really doing something, although when I did the result was most rewarding. The painted figures will stand competition from anything else on the market, and additionally have a particular charm of their own.

Every manufacturer seems to have a 'trade mark' on his product which is most likely due to the engraver putting his own stamp on the master. Historex figures, superbly engraved, are a shade 'wooden' and the faces, though beautifully detailed, and probably the nicest of all to paint, are somewhat characterless. Airfix are very full of animation, and so far show promise of a variety of 'types' as individuals.

On this criterion, SEGOM have a slight tendency to be youthful, but the range is a very nicely varied selection covering periods from the 17th century to the Second World War. All parts can be obtained separately and prices are most reasonable, being in the vicinity of 6op for foot figures or £1.25 for mounted, both being complete kits.

With a little care a first class figure can be produced from any kit. I substituted layered glued and painted cigarette paper for the belts and straps as I find this most convenient (two or three thicknesses of paper coated liberally with thinned styrene cement or, for SEGOM, thinned acetate). The thoughts of what can be done from the basic bits led of course to 'chopping' and here I used a combination of parts.

2nd Horse Cornette

Before we get too involved on this line let us take the actual figures converted. The first conversion was based on the mounted Musketeer of Louis XV period, which in itself is a most attractive figure. Looking through my various references I was struck by the fact that the basic style of dress was applicable to a wide range of soldiers—for example the Cuirassier of 1668, or the Cornette of the 2nd Horse illustrated in Funkens' *Costumes of all Times Vol I*. After a little more digging in references to see what confirmatory information was available, I decided to go for the 2nd Horse Cornette. The 2nd Regiment of Horse, the Queens, became the Kings Own in

1714, and so far as can be ascertained the 2nd had yellow facings until considerably later than this date when they should have changed to the Royal Blue. This must have led to some confusion because the 3rd, which became the 3rd Queens Horse, later the 2nd Dragoon Guards (the Queens Bays), wore buff and as the yellow worn was often a faded buff shade there could be confusion, so you can decide for yourself if your colour is the pale yellow of the 2nd Horse or the Buff of the 2nd DG, as the dress is generally suitable for either.

I suggest starting with a complete SEGOM kit of the musketeer as the bits not used will be very handy for future conversions, and a well-stocked 'bits box' is essential for anyone planning figure conversions as a hobby. It is always useful if a 'spare bit' which is nearly like that required can be found, but if none is available any scrap can be used. I look upon the parts as heads, legs, arms, bodies etc and simply 'mix' as required, adding or removing bits as necessary.

As I have a well-stocked spares box I selected items from this. They were as follows: saddle, Historex French saddle with cloth (84); legs, long riding boots (227); and pistol holsters (75) (the numbers are the Historex spares list numbers). I also used a Historex horse as I had other plans for the SEGOM one—this was purely a matter of choice, and any make can be used.

Step one is to fit the saddle on the horse—it may need a little shaping to sit right. The cloth lower edge is cut back at an angle tapered from zero at the front cutting close to the leather part of the saddle flap, tapering to the longest edge at the rear. The lower corner is rounded and two small tassels, fashioned from sprue or from the bits box, attached to the lower corner.

Next glue the legs together, seating them on the saddle to make sure they sit right. This is most important if your model is a mixture of different kits as they are not usually entirely compatible. The SEGOM body will not fit over the Historex legs so quite a bit of filing to the waist and lower body is needed until the fit is right. If you leave a couple of undercut notches after filing it will help fixing. A good blob of thick acetate glue made as SEGOM instructions in the body and a blob of styrene cement on the legs, fit the two together and leave to dry.

The next job is to fit the cuirass. Again it will not fit over the coat so the coat must be filed until it will fit. On my model I turned back the front skirts of the coat and fitted the skirts over the saddle. The acetate softens in hot water and is very easily worked.

Finally fit head, arms, etc. I used a scrap of tissue soaked in acetate glue to fill the gap between neck and cuirass, and represented a lace collar with this. I also used my pyrogravure at very low heat to work the rider's hair, and horse's mane and tail. This is an essential piece of equipment for a figure modeller working in any plastic.

Finally painting. The coat is Campaign Colours crimson, with cuffs and turnbacks in yellow/buff made from Humbrol Authentic colour Afrika Korps yellow with a touch of white and stone, a slight variation on this shade also being used on the pistol holsters. Breeches are buff (Campaign ochre with a touch of white and yellow), gloves light brown, cuirass bright with Pactra chrome, the saddle cloth gold lined out with white, blue and white with red diagonals, pistol holster lines white/blue/gold. For gold I use Florentine liquid gold leaf from Winsor & Newton, which is not cheap but my 75p bottle has been going two years and still hardly used from appearance. The colour is a scrap of old handkerchief frayed at the edges and soaked in polystyrene glue. It is painted buff/yellow with gold fringes and has the Queen's cypher 'CR' inside the garter. The garter is embroidered red, the rest gold. The sword is from the kit and carried on a white sash.

3rd Foot grenadier

The 17th Century infantry figure offers a large number of possibilities, since apart from simple changes of colour and detail, which can provide soldiers of a wide range of countries, the style of dress is similar for a fairly long and interesting period. My second conversion depicts a grenadier of the early 18th Century. The basic dress is similar, a long coat, a long inner coat, breeches and stockings, with or without gaiters. Accurate information on this period is scarce, and C. C. P. Lawson in his *History of the Uniforms of the British Army* comments on this fact. As with much of the early dress much information is dependent on contemporary paintings, and this leads to much doubt as to the accuracy of any specific 'fact'.

My model is based on certain assumptions and represents a grenadier of the 3rd Foot about 1750. Paper turned-back lapels have been added to the coat front, the tails turned back, and a tall mitre cap made from paper. The coat is red with buff turnbacks and cuffs, the cap a creamy buff embroidered with a black demi-griffin holding a battleaxe and a black grenade with red flames on the little flap. Breeches are buff with white stockings, but white, grey or black gaiters could be worn. The grenadier carries a large grenade pouch slung low on his right with a sword on his left. George II made serious efforts to standardise clothing in his army and a book was published with this object in 1742. Three known copies exist and a fourth is believed to be in the USA. Hand coloured plates show all the regiments.

Royal clothing warrants were issued in 1743 and 1749, but no copy has yet come to light, the earliest known being that of 1751, and this is frequently quoted as the uniform in being, whereas it was more likely the *intent* because many differences in dress from that laid down in the Warrant are known and proven to exist at a later date. However, though the accuracy of the figure modelled may be questionable, it is probably a case of 'my interpetation is as good as yours' and the grenadier looks very nice.

A Tudor duo

A developing interest in things military will usually lead to gaining some information on origins and it is almost certain that any modeller of historic figures will name the Yeoman of the Guard as the oldest British Army unit. Indeed the Yeomen are the oldest standing fighting force in any army, as they are known to have existed in 1485. A warrant dated September 16, 1485 is 'To John Frye, one of the Yeomen of the Guard'. Earlier bodyguard units had certainly existed . . . the House Carls of Edwin King of Northumbria, Edward II and his 'Garde du Corps du Roy', but these units were raised by individual sovereigns and disbanded at their deaths. In 1509, Hall's Chronicles record 'This yere the King ordered fiftie Gentle-menne to bee Speres, every of theim to have an archer, a demilaunce, a custrell, and every spere to have three great Horses, to bee attendaunt on his persone, of the whiche bende the erle of Exssex was Captain, and Sir Jhon Pechie Lieutenant . . .'. Ancient documents continue to record the existence of the 'Speres' and in 1539 Hall records dress livery for the 'Fifty Gentlemenne, called Pensioners or Speres', while in 1569 the Pensioners were mustered in Hyde Park before Queen Elizabeth. The Corps is now known as the Honourable Corps of Gentlemen at Arms.

However, back to the Tudor era, and neglected as it may be from the modeller's point of view the sight of SEGOM's Henri IV figure, which is perfect Tudor style, made modelling these ancient British soldiers a must.

To model a 'Spere' the basic figure is largely correct, and the main alteration is to provide a small conical hat, a cloak, and battleaxe. The Pensioners wore the colours of the House of Tudor, green and white. A painting in Milan shows Elizabeth with her Guard and they are wearing green doublet (slashed white?) with black cloaks lined crimson enriched with gold lace or embroidery, hose of yellowish-buff, and a pointed white cap with a gold band and a tuft of white feathers. The axe has a gilt head, the shoes are crimson, and the gloves medium brown with crimson fringe.

A Yeoman of the Guard figure needs rather more alteration. The 'Coatte' is longer, with a front slit to the waist and rounded edges to the slit. The popular Elizabethan 'puffed' sleeves are worn and the ruff is a different shape.

Fit the legs to the body and cut away the tunic below the waist. Replace with a tunic skirt shaped from paper or cloth soaked in liquefied acetate. Remove the chain and medallion, fit arms and build up the sleeves with Green Putty or similar. Position the head and when set trim the underside of the collar ruff to give the effect of a stiffened standing collar with the ruff at the top.

The flat hat is rather like a pill box and was made from a thin strip of plastic sheet glued round the head after the hair had been trimmed down, and a top from Green Stuff. The feather is a scrap of sprue worked with the pyrogravure.

The Rose and Crown motif is cut from thin plastic card or paper and glued to the chest. The coat is red with a black band edged yellow round the sleeve puffs, below the waist and round the lower edge of the tunic skirt. The body of the tunic is embroidered with a cross hatching of gold lace, and the rose and crown embroidered in gold and silver thread. The doublet is yellow slashed red, and the hose yellow. The shoes are black, the sleeves below the 'puffs' violet with white cuffs, the collar black and the ruff white. Gloves tan with red fringes. The sword, in a black scabbard, is suspended from a narrow gold belt, and the axe has a gilt head. With the similarity of dress for a wide range of Elizabethan costumes, this figure offers tremendous possibilities for conversions, as do many others in the SEGOM range.

five

Joe Gadd
Large-scale plastic figures

Many modellers prefer to work in the largest scale possible because of the fine detail which can be incorporated; and if you want to work in plastic then the choice is really limited to the range of 1:12 scale figure kits manufactured by Airfix. Many modellers scorn these kits as 'kid's stuff' without ever having taken the trouble to really examine them; and although most are rather stiff and doll-like, careful work and painting can produce some superlative figures, as shown here by Joe Gadd. Similarly, younger readers may like to attempt a conversion of one of these larger kits before moving on to the complexities of Historex or similar, because they are relatively cheap and because the parts are larger, easier to hold and easier to paint.

Elsewhere in this book you will find articles on painting and converting 54mm, and the even smaller 'wargame' figures, but to many people these models are too small or too tedious to work on. To those modellers the larger scale figures may be more practical and make a more rewarding pastime. The beauty of the larger figures is that they can be constructed to a high degree of military accuracy, or as purely decorative figures with enough detail to be recognisable. Some of the possibilities are shown in the photographs.

I have used as a basis for my conversions the Airfix range of 1:12 scale figures. They are cheap, easy to work with, and of course large enough to work on comfortably. Mention of decorative figures reminded me that I saw recently some China figures on sale in a large store retailing at about £50. Now using the Airfix kits you can produce comparable items for about 50p! No doubt the china things will last longer, and it is a matter of conjecture whether our plastic figures will be dug up in 500 years time to be cooed over as the china ones might, but you aren't going to spend hours of careful work on a model just to give it to little Willie to play with. With careful assembly then, and reasonable handling, there is no reason why your finished product shouldn't give years of pleasure. Some of my figures have been on display for a good many years now, and they are as good as the day they were made.

Having, I hope, aroused your interest, we can set about making a start on your new hobby. Like most projects you need to start with an idea of what you want to achieve. The range of military uniforms is a vast one, quite literally there are thousands to choose from. Some people concentrate on a particular period or war, currently the Napoleonic one is very popular because of the variety of the uniforms and the wealth of decoration on them, so you have plenty of scope in your choice. To a beginner, the Napoleonic dress might be just a little too elaborate, so to illustrate what can be done I have chosen a couple of British Army types from the 1914 period, and have appended more detailed instructions at the end of this article.

Let us assume that you have decided on what particular type or period you are going for. Your next step should be to arm yourself with some sort of reference book or pictures to guide you. With the great interest being shown in the subject nowadays, the literature available is quite astonishing, and to a newcomer very bewildering. It is quite easy to buy an expensive, lavishly illustrated book, only to find that when you come to consult it, it is quite useless for your purpose. So many of them show front or side views of a particular uniform, but hardly ever do they show the back. If they do show the back view, you can bet your boots they won't show the front! It therefore pays to be careful what you go for at first then.

I would heartily recommend Arthur Taylor's little book *Discovering British Military Uniforms* to you. At 30p it is a real bargain and it does give a wealth of detail (including back views). Of course as time goes by it is surprising how soon you can amass quite an impressive reference library of your own. Browsing around book shops, jumble sales and the like is always a good way of picking up useful material, even picture postcards can be useful. Most public libraries stock books on military subjects, and the local museum or Regimental depot is another happy hunting ground for the military modeller. I always take a small sketch book with me when visiting museums and the like to record the more intricate details of dress. It is surprising, when attendants or curators see someone taking more than just a passing interest, just how helpful they can be, and that little extra help can do wonders.

So far then we have established how to select the sort of thing we want to do and how to find reference books to guide us. What next? Well, we will need a tool kit of some sort. Now you can really splash out on a tool kit, and spend pounds on knives, files, clamps and all sorts of gadgetry. A matter of choice and depth of pocket of course, but you can start quite simply and cheaply.

The first requirement must be a good quality modelling knife, the best you can afford — cheap tools are never worth it. A good knife for trimming off 'flash marks' or reshaping should be regarded as an investment, and with care should give years of service. You'll need a small hacksaw, for cutting off unwanted parts too thick for your knife. A good one sufficient for our purpose can be bought quite cheaply in your nearest chain store.

For clamps, I'd suggest a few wooden clothes pegs, the spring type ones of course, since you can shape the ends of your pegs to suit any purpose, and they are quite strong enough to hold parts together while the cement dries or during painting.

Plasticine is an invaluable tool too, and comes in handy for a multitude of jobs. For example, a small blob with a match stuck in it makes a good holder for small parts being painted. A selection of elastic bands will always come in handy too, where your pegs are too small for holding.

For smoothing or sanding down, get yourself some manicurist's emery boards from Boots. The beauty of the emery boards is that you can cut them to any shape you want with a pair of scissors, and they have a coarse side and a smooth. With a shaped emery board you can get right into the most awkward places, and with the two grades of paper produce a good workmanlike finish.

Painting your models is an art in itself, so a few tips on that won't come amiss. Firstly, bearing in mind the golden rule, get the very best brushes you can afford, and look after them. The proper care and 'training' of your brushes will pay dividends in producing a really first class finish. Always make sure that you really get your brushes clean after use, and lay them down to dry on some newspaper. Don't make the mistake of thinking that you need a very thin brush to paint thin lines, you want a fairly fat brush for that, and you train it by shaping it between your fingers to a point when it is wet with white spirit or 'turps'. Properly trained, you will find it easy enough with a little practice to get those lines really neat.

Paints you buy as you need them, a wide choice is available in both matt and gloss, and there are one or two makers who produce 'authentic uniform colours'. By the way, you can always turn a matt paint into gloss by adding a touch of linseed oil. Buying your paints in those small tins is a very expensive way of buying paint, so do remember to get those lids back on tight. I usually squeeze them back on with the aid of a small vice. Nothing is more infuriating than finding that the paint you want to use next has gone hard in the bottom of the tin and the shops are shut.

The correct type of cement should be purchased when you buy your kits. After that you will need a tube of body putty for filling in and building up, and there's your tool kit complete.

You should now be ready to start. Assuming that you are going to follow one or both of my suggested conversions you will need the 1:12 scale Airfix Household Cavalry Trumpeter and the Coldstream Guardsman kits. The choice is yours of course, so you may decide to have a go at a figure of your own devising. In that case I've laid out a few tips in altering positions and general assembly that you may find useful.

Firstly you should make sure that you have got all the parts you require, and then put them into a logical assembly sequence, eg both parts of the arms and legs together and so on. I usually bash straight on and stick all the bits I want together, using plenty of cement at the joins and running it well into the inside seams as well, using a pointed match to work it well in. After cementing, clamp up with clothes pegs or elastic bands and leave for at least 24 hours to harden off. That way you will get a good strong assembly which will take a surprising amount of rough treatment. When dry you can then set about whatever alterations to the limbs etc you have decided on. Cleaning off the residue of cement or flash marks can be included in your tidying up operations when you have finished alterations.

To alter the position of the limbs is easy enough, merely cut away the locating pieces, move to the position required and cement into place. When dry, any protruding parts are then cut away, sanded down to match the profile of the body, and any holes or cracks exposed are then filled with body putty, which is again sanded down to suit when dry. If the holes are too big to fill in straight away, some plastic card stuck inside will provide an answer (see Fig 1).

It is not often that you will be content just to alter the position of a limb, you will want to alter its attitude as well. Just as easy, suppose you want to change an arm from being straight to bent at right angles, you would first carefully cut the arm at the elbow joint. Keep the elbow joint on the outside to maintain correct anatomical proportions.

Next cut some lengths of sprue (the scrap plastic which holds the kit parts together) to a little longer than you require. Bend the sprue to the required shape by holding it near a candle flame; this may take a bit of practice to achieve the desired result, but you will soon get the hang of it. When you have produced the shapes you want stick them into the upper arm, not forgetting to use plenty of cement. Set aside to dry, and then cut to correct length, build up to correct thickness with body putty, not forgetting to put creases in where necessary to simulate the folds of cloth (see Fig 2).

Similarly, when altering legs you use the combination of sprue and body putty. Other variations can be made of course by moving the heads around, and although alterations to the bodies are a bit trickier, if you use sprue or plastic card and your body putty techniques sensibly you can ring all sorts of changes. In Fig 3 I have suggested how you could alter a body slightly. Other ideas will obviously occur to you as you progress.

By the way, you can use melted scrap plastic to fill in large holes or to build up different helmets etc, but don't try this unless you have got plenty of ventilation. What you do is to shave down your scrap plastic into a tin lid and pour cement over it, stirring with a piece of wood until you produce a nice thick porridge. You will get an excellent filler that will set very hard and sand down well, but I must repeat that you need plenty of ventilation as it does give off very strong fumes which are not too healthy to breathe.

Having altered the limbs to your satisfaction, you can start to assemble your figure. Obviously the amount of care and attention you give to the job at this stage will determine the final standard. Do be careful then that all the parts fit snugly together before you cement, use plenty of cement and set aside to dry properly before you start sanding down the seams and joints. As mentioned earlier, you are bound to have one or two holes or cracks

Top *A selection of typical 20-25mm metal figures. From left to right the makers are Jacklex, Hinton Hunt, Warrior, Hinchliffe, Lamming and Phoenix.* **Above** *More 20-25mm figures from George Gush's collection. From left to right the manufacturers are Rose, Miniature Figurines, Alberken (or early 'Minifig'), Greenwood & Ball (new 25mm range), Tradition, Greenwood & Ball (early) and Almark. These two photos clearly show the widely differing styles and sizes available within this scale bracket.* **Below** *George Gush's Byzantine Emperor and standard bearer. The unpainted figures show the horse used, the original standard bearer figure and, at far right, the Hinchliffe senior Roman officer who has to undergo some rather painful surgery before becoming Emperor!*

Top *George Gush's English Civil War group showing a wounded officer receiving refreshment. The unpainted figures at left and right are the Hinchliffe officer and Lamming medieval artilleryman used in the conversion.* **Above** *30mm Tradition figures. At left is their old Guard Grenadier officer and at right the Empress' Dragoon. In the middle is Bruce Quarrie's early Polish Lancer conversion.* **Below** *30mm Tradition French Old Guard Horse Artillery officer, mounted trumpeter and Grenadier drummer.*

Above *Front and rear views of Bruce Quarrie's three 30mm conversions, the Chasseur à Pied, Old Guard sapper and blanketed 'retreat from Moscow' figure, construction of which is described in Chapter 7.* **Below** *The smallest figures which can be painted to a reasonable standard of detail are the 15mm products of Miniature Figurines and other makers. The 50p piece clearly shows off the size of these tiny French Napoleonic figures.*

Above *Front and rear views of Robert Gibson's 54mm metal figure animations and conversions. From left to right the photos show the uhlan officer, French dragoon, Prussian Reserve infantryman, Bavarian jäger and Hanoverian infantryman.* **Below** *the dismounted cavalry figure often shows the uniform and horse furniture to better advantage. Depicted are a Royal Horse Artillery trooper of 1812 (Kirk) and a trooper of Baylor's Dragoons in the normal regimental uniform worn on campaign (Lasset).*

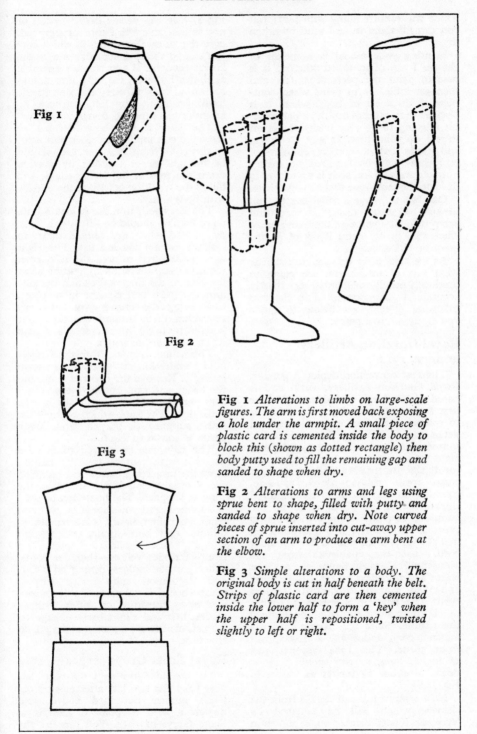

Fig 1

Fig 2

Fig 3

Fig 1 *Alterations to limbs on large-scale figures. The arm is first moved back exposing a hole under the armpit. A small piece of plastic card is cemented inside the body to block this (shown as dotted rectangle) then body putty used to fill the remaining gap and sanded to shape when dry.*

Fig 2 *Alterations to arms and legs using sprue bent to shape, filled with putty and sanded to shape when dry. Note curved pieces of sprue inserted into cut-away upper section of an arm to produce an arm bent at the elbow.*

Fig 3 *Simple alterations to a body. The original body is cut in half beneath the belt. Strips of plastic card are then cemented inside the lower half to form a 'key' when the upper half is repositioned, twisted slightly to left or right.*

which will require filling with putty but you can fill them in and sand off when dry.

Painting your model is a matter of choice. I am often asked whether it is best to paint the parts separately and then assemble, or to paint when complete. I do a bit of both, where it is obvious that, after assembly, a particular bit is going to be very tricky to get at, then I do paint first. In any event you will find that a certain amount of retouching will be required no matter how careful you are, so it is up to you to develop the technique that suits you best.

One last tip, have a small box by you to keep all those discarded parts and scrap bits. You will find them invaluable when making up extra items of equipment or filling holes etc.

As we said early on, you can decide what sort of model you are going to produce, purely decorative or strictly accurate. I have attempted in the two following conversions below to guide you along the two paths.

Royal Garrison Artillery gunner, 1914

The first conversion depicts a gunner, Royal Garrison Artillery, 1914, and is based on the Airfix Guardsman kit. The first step, after assembling the body, is to remove the buttons, epaulettes, and detail from skirt. You will need eight new buttons for the front of the jacket, and eight for the skirt. See Fig 4 and photos for details. Buttons are easily made from scrap sprue rubbed down to size, rounded off and sliced to the required thickness (Fig 5). Next, make up the ammunition pouch from 5 thou plastic card, as shown in Fig 6 and locate on belt as shown in the photos. For shoulder cords, use the epaulettes from the Household Cavalry figure reduced in width and thickness by sanding or filing and then shaped to simulate twisted cord. The bayonet is sheathed, so cut the bayonet from the rifle and remove the handle. Stick the handle into the bayonet frog, and shape a new sheath from sprue. The 1914 bayonet was 18 inches long, so you should scale it down to about 1½ inches as shown in Fig 7.

Now remove the cuff details from the sleeves, which will be replaced by 'Austrian Knots' painted on, as shown in

Fig 8. You can decide here whether or not to assemble the figure as supplied, ie in the 'at ease' position, in which case you can go ahead in accordance with the kit instructions. If you want to assemble as shown however, the right arm should be moved back to carry the rifle in the 'trail' position. The left arm can be assembled as supplied anyway.

The legs, if you have decided to assemble as supplied, can be fixed next. In this conversion, however, they should be brought closer together by shaving down the tops at the inside edges, and filling the resulting cracks on the outside with body putty.

The left hand, to make it look a little more lifelike, should be filled with body putty, and when dry sanded down to make a natural looking fist. The right hand is required to hold the rifle, so it requires some alteration by cutting away the tops of the fingers. Position the rifle into the palm and cement in to place, then using the fingers you cut away reposition them around the rifle. Use body putty to fill in any cracks, and sand down when dry to shape.

The helmet is made from the Household Cavalry kit, cut to shape as shown in Fig 9. Remove the decoration around the badge and rim, but leave the Garter Star and the embellishment around the spike hole. The knob which replaces the spike supplied is shaped from scrap sprue as shown in Fig 6.

The rifle can be altered to make a passable 1914 pattern type by cutting away the projecting barrel, and reducing the foresight guard slightly. Use the sling as supplied. The boots can be used as supplied, and you should be ready to paint your first figure. Colours are as follows: dark blue—tunic, trousers and helmet; scarlet—collar and piping on front of tunic; yellow—shoulder cords, collar grenade badges, piping on collar, cuff decoration and service stripes; black—boots, metal parts of rifle; brown —wooden furniture on rifle; white— gloves, belt and sling; brass—badge on helmet, chin strap, buttons, and plate on rifle butt.

Royal Scots Greys sergeant, 1914

My second figure uses the parts left over from the two kits after making the RGA gunner described above, and depicts a Staff Sergeant of the Royal Scots Greys in 1914. You can use the

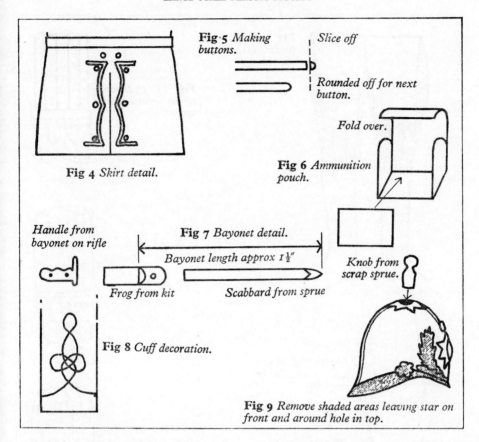

Fig·5 Making buttons.

Slice off

Rounded off for next button.

Fig 4 Skirt detail.

Fold over.

Fig 6 Ammunition pouch.

Handle from bayonet on rifle

Fig 7 Bayonet detail.

Bayonet length approx 1½"

Knob from scrap sprue.

Frog from kit

Scabbard from sprue

Fig 8 Cuff decoration.

Fig 9 Remove shaded areas leaving star on front and around hole in top.

parts from the Household Cavalry kit as they are, in which case you will end up with a figure which is near enough, but not strictly accurate. For example, the figure shown in the photos is wearing the bearskin cap supplied with the kit, but I have included instructions for making up a more realistic one. Similarly, you can use the sword sling provided, but it is quite easy to replace it with your own made up from card.

The first step is to assemble the body in accordance with instructions supplied, then using the techniques already described, straighten the right arm as shown in the photos and, when assembling to body, move it slightly back to the rear. The left arm can be used as instructed in the kit.

Remove the tops of the figure's boots to just below the knee, then, using scrap sprue, assemble the boots to the legs. When dry fill in with body putty, filling

out the sides of the breeches to simulate riding breeches as worn (Fig 10).

Cut away the handle of the sword from the scabbard. Make up sword blade from scrap and assemble it with handle and guard supplied. Do make sure your blade will fit the scabbard. Next assemble the right hand, cementing the sword handle into the palm before putting the two parts together, then make up two sword slings from microstrip or 5 thou card. Fix the sword slings through rings on scabbard, and assemble left hand, cementing the scabbard into the palm locating between the rings. When the hands are dry, assemble to arms. You can fill in the left hand with putty, sanding down when dry to give a better looking fist. Assemble arms to body; the slings are cemented to belt, one just to the left of the belt buckle, the other to the rear of the belt.

If you wish to use the bearskin cap

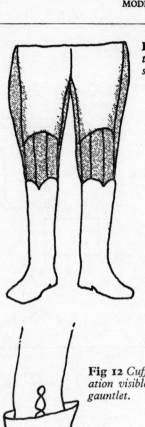

Fig 10 *Body putty to be added where shaded.*

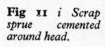

Fig 11 *i Scrap sprue cemented around head.*

ii Strips of card cemented around sprue.

Fig 12 *Cuff decoration visible under gauntlet.*

iii Cover with body putty scored to simulate fur. Overall height should be $1\frac{1}{4}''$.

Fig 14 *Gold crown outlined with black. White eagle outlined with black. Gold chevrons with scarlet in between.*

iv Add hackle on left approximately $\frac{3}{4}''$ long. Score chin strap to simulate chain.

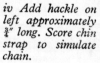

Fig 13

supplied, assemble in accordance with the instruction, but remove the plume on the right hand side, make good with putty, scoring with a knife to blend in with the fur. Make up a new hackle with putty on the left of the cap. The hackle was ten inches long so you will need to scale down to about ¾ inch or so. To make up a more suitable cap follow instructions in Fig 11. Finally, make up replacement shoulder tabs with scrap card. The pouch and spurs can be fitted as supplied. Note that when assembling the arms and legs, you should try to achieve an alert looking pose, as if the soldier has just drawn his sword in alarm.

For decorative purposes use gloss paint all over, otherwise follow the guide below. The cuff decoration was a rather elaborate Austrian Knot, but as the figure is wearing gauntlets, very little of the knot can be seen (see Fig 12): matt black—bearskin cap, top of scabbard; gloss black—boots and pouch; blue—breeches, collar and shoulder tabs; yellow—stripe on breeches, piping on collar and shoulder tabs, cuff decoration; white—hackle, belts, slings, gauntlets, eagle badges on collar and over chevrons on right arm (Fig 13); brass—buttons, chin strap; gold—chevrons and crown on arm (Fig 14); silver—sword and scabbard.

SECTION TWO

Introduction

The history of model figures cast in metal is a very old one, dating back to the 18th Century at least and the beautifully animated two-dimensional or 'flat' figures produced by a number of continental manufacturers. These were prize items which could only be purchased by the wealthy and the aristocracy, and surviving examples today fetch enormous prices at auctions.

The origins of the modern metal figure can really be traced, however, to the hollow-cast models manufactured by Britains from the 1890s, which many readers will recall from childhood.

Britains were the first manufacturers of three-dimensional (or 'round') figures to standardise on a scale, and it is this same scale of 1:32 or 54mm which has subsequently been adopted by practically every other manufacturer as a standard.

The relatively crude and simplified products made by Britains in those early days bear little resemblance to the masterpieces of sculpture being turned out by a vast number of craftsmen/manufacturers today. These are usually solid-cast figures and in most cases are superbly detailed down to the last button and thread of uniform braid. They are available in kit form or as ready assembled models which merely require painting, and the range available covers practically every nationality and historical period you can think of, from ancient Greek and Roman warriors to American GIs.

Hand in hand with the 54mm scale figures produced since the last war has grown up another range of popular models to a smaller 30mm scale. It was the availability of these figures, nearly half the size of their 54mm counterparts but still beautifully detailed, which gave the first real impetus to the now rapidly growing hobby of wargaming. They can be painted relatively quickly, and are small enough to organise into miniature units which can march and countermarch across a fairly small table top.

The next significant development was the birth of the 20mm figure, half the size again of a 30mm but still well animated and detailed, which was especially effective when grouped in large numbers and gave still further impetus to the hobby of wargaming. Since then the emphasis has changed slightly following the introduction a few years ago of an in-between scale, 25mm. These figures are sufficiently larger than 20mm to allow a considerable amount more detail to be incorporated, but are still sufficiently smaller than 30mm to render them preferable to wargamers.

Moving right up the scale, the last few years have seen the advent of several ranges of really large metal model figures in 75, 77, 90 and 120mm scales. These vary in quality from really superlative animations with bags of character to perfectly moulded but rather lifeless 'uniform dummies' and are, of course, rather more expensive than their smaller counterparts. The chief advantage of larger models is all the additional fine detail which can be incorporated; but the expense incurred in purchasing a figure can be daunting to the most ardent conversion and animation enthusiast!

Conversions and animations of metal-cast figures are really no more difficult than with plastics nowadays, since with the arrival of quick-drying epoxy resins and products such as Plastic Metal there is no real need for an any-more elaborate tool kit, and most of the actual techniques are very similar. It merely requires a little more elbow-grease to cut through half an inch of metal than half an inch of plastic. In the following chapters, several well-known authors explain their own methods of tackling animations and conversions using metal figures, so if you've never tried, now is the time to begin; while if you have tried, you will still pick up some useful labour-saving techniques if nothing else; and probably learn how to improve your own standards as well.

six

George Gush
Metal 'wargames' figures

In this chapter, well-known Airfix Magazine *contributor George Gush describes some of the advantages and disadvantages of metal figures in the small 20/25mm scales. These are essentially wargames figures, where the emphasis is generally on appearance en masse, and George outlines some suggestions to speed up the painting of groups of figures—a time-consuming and frequently tedious task. He also shows how some simple but effective conversions can be rendered, either to lend added interest and personality to a wargames army, or for incorporation in a diorama.*

Round figures in these scales have been about for some time, the famous firm of Heyde being an early producer of rather charming little half-round figures. In the 20th Century they have been linked to the popular 00 model railway scale, as 54s were to the earlier 0 Gauge. In England 1:72 scale model aircraft gave rise to the Skybird range of figures before the Second World War, and this range—'modern' British and German figures—could still be purchased on their cards after the war.

Also in the early post-war years, W. Y. Carman produced a few 20mm half-round figures, and I recall gazing, in Hamley's, at beautiful painted Greenwood and Ball figures—at 'collector' prices, alas.

The 1960s, however, was the real decade of the small figure, its rise linked to the gradual spread of wargaming; Rose Models and Norman Newton were early in the field, the latter with the beautiful 1-inch Crimea range (now happily revived in the new Tradition range). Marcus Hinton's Hinton Hunt 20mm range was the most prolific in this early period, with a fine choice of Napoleonics still growing today.

By 1964 Scruby in America and Aylmer in Spain were offering 20mm figures sometimes seen in this country, and this year also saw the appearance of the short-lived Alberken concern, which by 1965 had come into the control of Neville Dickinson (in those days they had offered painted armies of over 120 pieces for ten guineas!). This, the birth of Miniature Figurines, unquestionably the largest producer today, was perhaps the start of the huge boom which has transformed the market since; not only new figures but new firms have come thick and fast—Garrison, Douglas, Phoenix, Lamming, Hinchliffe, Warrior, Jacklex, Tradition et al.

Today, the 20/25mm boom is still under way, and the great feature of this scale is the quite extraordinary number and variety of figures which can be purchased 'off the shelf'—a Turkish 16th Century Spahi, Darius on his throne, a Pictish bowman or a Band of the Old Guard, a Panzer Grenadier or a Cheyenne Dog Soldier and just about anything in between, and the general standard of figures increases almost daily; a happy state of affairs undreamed of when my own collection started.

Perhaps the only fly in the ointment is the persistent disagreement among makers as to what 20mm and 25mm scales actually are!

The makers

Garrison an early 20mm Ancient and Napoleonic range in a hard alloy and rather 'flat' positions; being replaced by a superb new 25mm range (only disadvantage—they are hard to fit on the bases used by most wargamers).

Hinchliffe extraordinarily high casting standards in this large range (Second World War, American Civil War, Colonial, Napoleonic, English Civil War and Ancient). Fine animation and detail, and the best horses in the business. Occasional anatomical oddities, and many are in a 'large' 25mm scale so won't easily mix with other makers' figures (at least in the same unit).

Hinton Hunt very characteristic figures though the style is hard to describe exactly. 20mm—fit in with early Garrison. Huge Napoleonic range, also ECW, Ancients, ACW, and Colonial.

Jacklex attractive, genuine 20mm figures, rather like early Greenwood and Ball; fit in with Airfix 20mm but smaller than the other figures here listed. ACW, Colonial and Ancient.

Lamming 25mm, fitting with Warrior and Minifigs. Sturdy-looking figures with good detail, some good horses, and I think the best Napoleonic artillery; besetting sin big heads on a few figures. Napoleonic range, being supplemented by splendid Medievals, and Ancients.

Miniature Figurines around 2,000 figures, periods 1870, ACW, Napoleonic, 18th Century, ECW, 16th Century, Medieval, Dark Ages, Ancients, Colonial, American War of Independence, and Indian wars, Jacobite Risings and Lord of the Rings—what can one say? 25mm, fitting with Lamming, Warrior, Phoenix 25mm, later Garrison. Very consistent high standard and excellent proportions.

A rather smooth and 'bland' style with little facial detail and sometimes a little stereotyped in position, but a great range.

Phoenix few, but very good, 25mm Napoleonics, 20mm ECW etc.

Rose a small range of ACW and Napoleonic figures—small, neat 20mms.

Tradition recently introduced range. The Stadden figures are outstanding though a little formal in style and pose; one or two of the others look a little undernourished; good detail. ACW, Crimea, Colonial, Napoleonic, 18th Century, Ancient. 25mm; could fit well with Hinchliffe *and* Minifigs.

Warrior sizeable range; many Napoleonics, also ECW, 16th Century and Ancient. 25mm; fit Minifigs etc; lively and rugged-looking though some early figures a little rough; recent ones have good detail; cheaper than most, at the time of writing at least.

Painting

There are probably at least nine-and-sixty ways of painting 20/25mm figures, and I must echo Kipling and admit that every single one of them is right. However, it would be impossible to cover all of them here, so I have concentrated on my own methods, with an occasional mention of the alternatives. Much written about working in other scales would apply here too, so I shall try to emphasise those methods especially applicable to the smaller figures, related, firstly, to smallness, which restricts very elaborate techniques and allows shortcuts which might not work on larger figures; and, secondly, to the fact that the 20/25mm, like his real-life original, is most often seen 'en masse'. Cost and size fit him for such a role, which both permits and demands reasonably quick and simple painting techniques.

The first job is to prepare the figures for painting. A sharp modelling knife is the best tool to remove flash, backed up by some cheap Woolworth's files (good enough for work on lead), small enough to get into the nooks and crannies of 25mm equipment; perhaps also a large flat file to clean the underside of the base. I also keep an old toothbrush to remove the sawdust in which some figures are packed.

Though some people get good results by painting on to bare metal, I consider undercoating essential—it guards against 'lead disease', makes the colours brighter and more solid, and makes the final finish more durable. The ideal under-coat is matt white universal primer, available in aerosols from Halfords or similar shops; you can line up a mass of figures and cover the lot in a few seconds, and it is very quick-drying.

For good results, one must use water colour brushes of at least 'Student' quality, obtainable from any art shop; they are *not* cheap but will last a fair time if cleaned and put away when not in use; don't use them for getting paint out of pots or for mixing—I keep a few old brushes for these jobs. Sizes oo, o and 1 are those required.

Paint is a more debatable matter; oils, acrylic paints and poster paints all have their advocates, but I think ordinary enamels are hard to beat for range, price, availability and wearing qualities—the latter important for wargames or 'parade' figures, as so many in this scale are. (There are some odd gaps in the enamel field though—why no matt dark red?—and why no matt grass-green, needed for bases?)

Even using enamels, there is still a choice of finish—you can use gloss, you can use matt, and you can finish off with matt or gloss varnish. I would certainly paint with matt in general—its quick drying is vital when you are doing a whole batch of figures; and personally I prefer to leave figures unvarnished, with the most natural possible appearance. I find they stand wargame use if mounted in groups to avoid unnecessary handling, and well undercoated; however, varnish can look good and gives the strongest finish, but do let the paint harden fully before applying varnish.

Painting techniques are obviously similar to those used on larger figures, but usually modified by the demands of small size and 'mass production'.

If you are doing a unit or army it is best to paint figures in batches, applying each colour to each figure in turn; the batch should be large enough for the first to be dry when you return to it, but not so large as to involve too much boring repetition; from ten to 30 is about right. I don't recommend sticking figures to a base or handle while painting—more trouble than it's worth—but usually leave bases and projections like bayonets till last, so there is something to hold the figure by.

When painting a lot of figures it is an idea to do a little 'production engin-eering'—working out in what order to apply colours. The larger areas will be painted first, with only enough care to avoid bare patches (look at the figure from several angles before going on, since it's easy to miss undercuts in this scale).

It may next be possible to fill in other areas not in touch with the first: for example, a Napoleonic infantryman gets his red coat; his black shako could be slopped on next, while the red was still wet, and later careful painting of face and collar will take care of any overlaps. Never be careful where you don't have to be, where subsequent painting will hide irregularity.

Make sure your order makes things easy for you: for example, I normally paint faces almost last (because it is easier to paint hands onto a musket than a musket *round* already-painted hands, and hands and faces must be painted at the same time to save remixing paint). However, where a wide-brim hat or helmet is worn, do the face first, probably splodging pink on the headgear—which your *subsequent* painting of the hat will cover without any extra labour on your part.

While on faces, the only ready-mixed colour suitable for Europeans is Testor's 'Flat Light Tan', and I recommend a mix of white with quite a lot of Airfix M1 Brick Red and a little yellow; Humbrol Authentic 'Leather' is quite good for Indians and similar. Mouths are done with flesh plus a little Airfix M12 Red, and eyes just indicated with a streak of brown are quite effective in

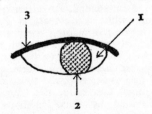

Method of painting eyes on a 20/25mm figure. 1 first paint white spot. 2 then eye dot (dark brown or blue) and 3 dark brown line.

this scale; I go a little further, using the technique illustrated which gives as good an impression as more elaborate methods in such a small size. The best 'general' colour for hair and eyes is dark brown (eg Humbrol Authentic Dark Wood) but I use black for Indians, Assyrians and so on, and a few redheads (MI again) and blondes improve the appearance of many units; blue eyespots are remarkably effective with the latter.

Shading, highlighting and outlining

You will have seen these techniques described elsewhere. Do we use them on the 25mm figure, especially when he is just one of a unit? My own line is to confine highlighting to very dark colours which cannot be shaded, and to flesh on figures which are showing a lot of it. Outlining can be very effective, especially on the smaller 20mm figures. It is best done in a very dark brown or grey, and I prefer a brush to the mapping pen sometimes used; however, I prefer shading, which is really a more naturalistic technique.

It must be said that neatly-painted figures with no such trimmings can look excellent in this small scale, but I think that if you have the time shading is worthwhile; on these small figures it does not have to be particularly accurate to give an excellent impression. I use it, firstly, with largish plain areas of colour which would otherwise look rather flat, secondly, on white areas, which seem to need it; and thirdly, where it is needed to indicate detail. Thus an Ancient Gaul in tunic and cloak would be shaded, a Napoleonic with his tunic covered with straps and equipment would not—but if he wore white breeches or had white belts passing across white lapels, these areas would be shaded. An alternative, if you use white undercoat, is Peter Gilder's method of wiping away paint so that the undercoat shows beneath it at the high points—quick and very effective, especially on horses, but very well moulded figures are required to make it look its best. Generally, the 'quality' effect obtained by these methods is disproportionate to the fairly minor trouble involved. Except where Peter's method can be used, I do not usually highlight horses, as I find a straightforward semi-matt finish (mixing matt and gloss paint) gives a good impression without it. (Incidentally, I find it pays when painting cavalry to start with the saddlecloth and then paint away from it in both directions, horse and man; it is really best to attach man to horse *after* painting.)

Converting and animating

Again resemble in most ways the methods used with larger figures, but with 20/25mms the *need* for conversions is much less in view of the enormous range of figures available—annoying to spend a hundred man hours turning Napoleonic Bashkirs into Mongols, only to have someone bring out Mongol figures next month. Thus the main requirement for conversions is probably from the diorama-maker, while the wargamer would chiefly be concerned with individuals like generals and standard bearers (even here you can buy ready-made a range of personalities from Alexander the Great through Cromwell to an endless list of Napoleonic commanders!). In the examples which follow I have taken these factors into consideration.

Much can be done in this small scale without any surgery at all, simply bending limbs which in a larger scale would need to be cut and reset (the hardness of the alloy used varies from maker to maker, so be cautious). This is especially useful with homecast figures, allowing a single spreadeagled figure to take up a vast range of positions.

Weapon-swapping is a frequent requirement and again simple in this scale; many collectors like to replace rather overscale lead pikes and spears—best for this is softish iron wire from garden shops or ironmongers, which can be hammered flat at the 'head' and filed to a point. Standard pins, decapitated, make good javelins, and can be flattened for use as a sword, with guard of foil from a toothpaste tube. Simple musical instruments such as horns can be made by heating, stretching and bending the 'sprue' from plastic kits; while sets of plastic accessories for 1:76 scale tank kits are a useful source of modern tools and weapons.

All are best attached with the quick-drying epoxy resin glues now available; I don't see any advantage in soldering which is even more 'fraught' with these tiny figures than it is with the 54s. When fitting, file a deep 'V' in the hand so that the weapon rests in and not on it, and be sparing with glue to avoid the appearance of a giant, blobby 'fist'. It is a good idea to rotate the weapon in the hand before settling it into place, to ensure good contact. Plasticine lumps will support the whole job while it sets. (Hinchliffe, Phoenix and Hinton Hunt produce figures with separate wire spears and lances already.)

Byzantine Emperor and Standard Bearer

At the time of writing no commander is available for the Byzantine armies which are as successful on the wargames table as they were in the dark ages, when they were the only disciplined troops in the western world. Byzantine officers wore costumes based on ancient Roman models, and I selected the Hinchliffe Roman Senior Officer as the basis for this figure. He has the right costume (except that his legs should be in trousers—just a matter of painting) and his position is suitable; free right arm which can be bent out to hold a spear, left across his body with his cloak looped over it, hand just right to hold a horse's reins. He could remain bareheaded, but I decided to give him an Imperial diadem, formed from a band of tooth-paste tube wrapped round the head and filled with epoxy resin; dangling ropes of pearls are twisted strips of the same material.

Next, he must mount his horse—not feasible for a foot figure in a larger scale

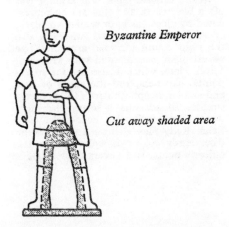

Byzantine Emperor

Cut away shaded area

without major conversion. In the present case, surgery is simple (if painful); his stand is carefully cut away, using an

Exacto Razor-saw (a most useful tool for all such jobs), and a V-shaped cutaway made in the figure as shown in the diagram; feet are tidied with a file and set in a suitable position, and fuse wire loops are glued about them as stirrups.

Next the horse: several mounts would be suitable, and the only contemporary pictures I know show them in leather and metal harnessing, but there are references to purple trappings, and I wanted something a little more spectacular for my commander, so decided to use a Miniature Figurines Medieval horse in cloth barding. The only modifications made were to cut down the high medieval saddle a little, and to file away both sides at this point, giving a rather 'wasp-waisted' effect. This allows the rider to fit and doesn't show on the finished model.

When fitted in place the figure receives a wire spear, and a strip of foil joins the cast reins on the horse to the rider's left hand.

Painting is mainly in purple and gold (a nice purple can be made with Airfix M12 red and Humbrol matt blue No 25). Saddle and boots are semi-gloss red (only the Emperor was allowed to wear red boots). The cloak is pale blue (used by Byzantine Guard units) and the horse is a grey (often reserved for generals and commanders in ancient times). Horse trappings are decorated with gold Chi-Ro monograms like that on the standard. Jewels are indicated with tiny drops of gloss red and green.

The accompanying standard-bearer is a very simple modification of a Miniature Figurine's Byzantine Dragon standard bearer; his original standard is cut away and replaced by a plain pike (obtainable from Warrior Metal Miniatures); a crossbar from a spare bit of pike has previously been glued across a notch cut in this, and a banner attached. This is simply paper, folder over the bar and glued with Uhu. I find paper the most satisfactory material for flags on figures which are to be handled; it should be attached before undercoating which helps to strengthen and stiffen it. The very fine linen used by draughts-men could be a better substitute if you can get it. The disc at the top is cut from plastic card with an office punch, while the tassels at the bottom are knots of a kind of nylon cord sold for kit strings—very handy stuff which also makes good tassels and cords for Napoleonic flags. The banner is purple with gold lettering, its bearer has a white tunic, light blue cloak, usual Byzantine red-brown trousers and yellowish boots, and wears a bronze helmet. (An effective way to paint bronze armour is to use Airfix G15 Bronze with a little G4 Black added; resultant dark bronze is highlighted along mouldings and other raised points with gold paint.)

English Civil War group

This was made as part of a small diorama, and represents a wounded Roundhead officer being assisted by his servant. I actually got the idea on seeing the latter figure, Lamming Medieval Artilleryman MF VII. He is kneeling to fire his gun in an attitude suited to supporting a casualty, and doesn't really need much conversion. I filed off his hood, added a wire guard to his sword-hilt, and cut off the top of his head to fit a plumed hat from a Warrior pikeman; such hat swaps are very easy in this small scale, the glue hiding any crack provided the surfaces are reasonably flat. His wide collar is just painted on (another bonus of 25mm scale) and I have edged it with a dark line to give an illusion of relief. His left arm, which is to support the wounded man's head, only had to be bent down a little but the hand is a fist, and I wanted it open; again a short-cut is possible in this scale: just *squash* the hand with pliers, then trim it to size with a file. The right arm had to be sawn free from the body and bent upward; the hand was treated like the left and a 'bottle' attached, which is being lifted to the officer's lips (it is a green glass bottle, made from a clear plastic cocktail stick, with Airfix G11 Crimson wine).

The officer is a Hinchliffe ECW figure. He first has his feet very carefully sawn from his stand, trimmed up, and set with pliers in a natural position for a man lying down. As his upper half will be supported clear of the ground, he must be bent, and this is achieved by a cut just below his sash, $\frac{2}{3}$ of the way through his body; he is bent and the remaining crack filled with glue—quite major changes in 25mm body positions can be made by this means, any traces being filed away after the glue has had a day or so to harden. Arms and hands are dealt with similarly to those of the other figure, and sword and scabbard are freed to lie at realistic angles on the ground. I cut the sword blade at an angle, to make it appear broken. His head had to come right round and up to bring his lips toward the proffered bottle, and this meant sawing it off, filing a flat in a new position, and glueing it back in its new place, with a little filing to adjust the collar to this.

Painting of this group would be largely a matter of taste, those being pre-uniform days, though the officer has an orange sash to indicate his Parliamentarian sympathies. I also made his face a much paler shade of flesh than usual.

He wears a corselet and helmet, and there are several ways of dealing with armour: an effective bright steel can be made with gloss black and silver—more of the former. Unless Testor black is used the colours tend to separate out a little, but this is rather effective, the black settling in depressions and outlining the separate plates. Alternatively there is a Steel in the Humbrol Railway range (R217), which can be very effective if highlighted with silver.

In the English Civil War armour was often blackened, and this can be represented by gloss black, or semi-matt black, or Airfix G16 Gunmetal (which is also the right colour for mail armour). The sword blade was painted with Humbrol Silver Plate, which I also use for spear-points, bayonets, and the edges of axes and similar weapons; Airfix G8 is pretty similar. 'Bloodstains' here and elsewhere were made with the ever-useful M1 Brick Red, plus a little scarlet. Some dark earth colour is splashed on the officer's boots, and covers their soles.

seven

Bruce Quarrie
30mm 'diorama' figures

I must confess to a personal bias in favour of the 30mm figure. To my mind a model in this scale combines all the advantages of larger, 54mm, or smaller, 20-25mm, figures, with none of their disadvantages. Certainly many of the figures being produced in this scale today fall little short of the miraculous in their animation and detail. Anyway, for those of you who are interested, here's how I go about my 'thing'. And if you've never tried a 30mm model, do have a go.

Younger modellers entering the sphere of figure modelling today have a tendency to regard 30mm scale as something of an anomaly, for the figures are neither compatible with normal 25mm wargames armies nor the popular 54mm collectors' size. However, until a few years ago 30mm was probably equal in popularity to 54mm, and there are still a number of advantages to working in this scale.

The 30mm 'round' figure, as manufactured by Tradition, Suren and Minot, to name the top three manufacturers today, evolved originally from the Continental 'flat' and 'half-round' figures which have been manufactured commercially since the 18th Century and have always enjoyed widespread popularity with diorama constructors. And this, indeed, is the main reason for their continued popularity among serious modellers today, for the figures are sufficiently large and well-detailed to permit painting up to almost 54mm standard, yet at the same time sufficiently small to allow their grouping in large numbers for diorama purposes.

Before the advent of the small 20/25mm figure, 30mm was also the scale used by the majority of wargamers in Britain—a very select band until about ten years ago—and despite the obvious wargames advantages of the smaller figures, it is still worth contemplating 30mm if you are a wargamer working in a period where the units can be kept fairly small; or similarly, if you like to see your wargames figures really well painted and detailed as individual 'men' rather than regimental blocks whose individual colouring is unimportant so long as the overall effect is right.

Collectors who specialise in superbly detailed, animated and painted individual display figures or small groups can also reap benefits from 30mm, since as I have already said the basic figures in most cases are sufficiently well defined to permit their painting to the highest standards. At the same time their small size means that more of them can be displayed in a given area, which is a great advantage if your display space is limited.

Despite this, most modellers will find the greatest benefits of 30mm lie in diorama construction, in which they will be helped by the extremely large and varied range of figures available. A visit to Edward Suren's shop at 60 Lower Sloane Street, London SW1 (on the way to the National Army Museum, so there's a good opportunity here to kill two birds with one stone if your time in London is limited) will show the sort of thing which can be achieved, while Tradition, 188 Piccadilly, London W1, usually have a couple of dioramas as well as individual figures on display.

At the time of writing the 'Willie' range, designed by Edward Suren and cast in pure tin (which accounts for their relatively high prices) is the largest in this scale. The range includes troops of the Roman Empire, Normans and Saxons of 1066, Renaissance, English Civil War and Marlburian periods, Seven Years War, early and late Napoleonic, Crimean and Franco-Prussian Wars and, perhaps the nicest series, a variety of late 19th Century Colonial troops including British and Highlanders, Zulus, Indians, Dervishes, Fuzzy-Wuzzys and Sikhs. There are also some attractive 'one off' figures including a Barbary Coast pirate, Blackamoor servant and a variety of girls!

The Tradition range, designed by Charles Stadden (who else?) is smaller but also cheaper, and being cast from a softer metal the figures lend themselves more than the Willie ones to conversion and animation (tin being rather hard and brittle to work with). The Tradition range incorporates more Napoleonics, including some really superb French Old Guard figures, Second World War British and Germans, American Civil War and some very attractive American War of Independence troops.

The Minot range is a fairly recent contender on the English market and has been specifically designed with the diorama constructor in mind. At the time of writing all the figures are Waterloo-period Napoleonics, and include some delightful ready-made groups including such items as troopers helping a wounded comrade off the field. Unfortunately the Minot figures are much more slightly proportioned than those in the corresponding Tradition and Willie ranges, so that although they are the same height they appear visually somewhat smaller. However, some of the wounded or 'dead' figures can be fitted quite happily into dioramas using Tradition or Willie soldiers since dead bodies have a tendency somehow to look smaller than when they were alive, as any combat soldier will confirm. One word of warning when incorporating this type of feature into a diorama, however: don't overdo the 'blood'. Nothing ruins the effectiveness of an otherwise well-constructed and painted diorama more than vast splashes of red paint everywhere!

Roy Dilley covers diorama construction more fully in a later chapter, so all I will say on the subject here is, don't overcrowd the scene with too many figures: a dozen or so well-animated models, positioned carefully so that they are artistically related to each other, is far more effective than 30 or 40 figures crammed into the same area.

Tools and materials

The tools and materials needed for working on 30mm metal figures are much the same as those required for 20/25mm or 54mm, and I manage quite satisfactory with the following, which I consider a minimum list:

Junior 6″ hacksaw; a selection of files ranging from the tiny Historex mousetail to a large, coarse model for removing gross detail; modelling knife and a selection of gouges (the Humbrol Multicraft tool chest provides an ideal range); soldering iron, five-minute epoxy resin and Plastic Padding. The latter I use for all 'building' work on metal figures, especially items such as fur busbies, hair, beards etc, since it bonds better with metal than Green Stuff or Body Putty, and dries out quite quickly into a rock-hard consistency which can be cut, filed and carved with the greatest of ease and no fears of shredding or cracking.

Ordinary Plasticine, after sealing with Humbrol Banana Oil or simple coating with polystyrene cement is also useful, especially for building up items of clothing as in the Polish lancer conversion described later. Tweezers for holding small components, a miniature vice, and the usual assortment of wire, paper, plastic card, rod and strip, Sellotape and Masking Tape are also necessary.

Conversion techniques

The first requirement before beginning any conversion is a clear idea of what you want to achieve. This sounds so obvious you may think it hardly worth stating, but it is astonishing how many modellers begin work on a model without any formed idea of what they are trying to achieve, and end up with a figure which, although perfectly detailed and painted so far as uniform is concerned, is anatomically incorrect to a greater or lesser degree! So the keynote is planning. Before you even touch the figure you are going to convert, make sure you have a print or illustration showing the pose you are going to attempt. If you can't find one, get a member of the family or friend to pose in the required stance and take photographs or do quick sketches from front, back and each side. That way, no matter how contorted the position you are aiming at, you can be certain it is *possible*. The same applies to horses, of course, and in this context 'Mac' Kennaugh's chapter on horse animation will help you achieve anatomically correct animals.

Generally speaking, relaxed, non-violent poses tend to look more realistic than contorted 'action' figures, for the simple reason that what you are doing in any model figure or diorama is encapsulating a tiny moment of time. As a result, the more animated the pose of a figure, the more the onlooker feels there is something 'wrong' since the figure *ought* to be moving. Thus the more violent the animation, the more care you must take to balance the figure in its surroundings and against other figures to minimise this effect.

Having chosen your figure and worked out the pose, the next requirement is a basic model to work from. By and large it doesn't matter what uniform or headgear the figure is wearing since this sort of surface detail can easily be removed and new detail added. What does matter is trying to find a figure whose basic stance is as close as possible to that you require, so as to eliminate as much as possible of the tedious work of altering head, torso and limb positions by cutting and filling.

The second thing to try to avoid is the necessity for using parts (limbs especially, although heads are not too much bother) from different models to form one composite figure. Not only does this double the amount of cutting work involved, with its attendant dangers of spoiling fine detail, but frequently arms and legs are of different lengths and girths even among figures from the same range by one manufacturer, and look out of place when transposed.

Having chosen a figure in as near as possible the pose you want, examine it carefully to see what detail items can be incorporated in your new model, and what will have to be removed or replaced. Small details can be protected while you cut and file at the rest of the figure by covering them with epoxy resin before you start work. This dries to form a protective covering over the detail in case your knife or file slips, yet can be peeled off quite easily later to reveal the intact detail underneath. I always cover the whole of a figure's face in this way at the very least.

Now plan your cuts carefully and mark the position of each with the tip of your knife blade or the point of a pair of compasses: this gives a guideline for your saw when you begin to cut and helps minimise 'skidding'. Bend limbs, weapons etc out of the way, clamp the figure firmly in the vice by its base, and begin to saw. Use firm, slow strokes of the blade in preference to going at it as if it were a block of firewood, and aim for a smooth, even cut.

The same applies to filing off surface detail, which should always be done *after* any cutting work is complete since the cutting will have removed parts of the figure which would otherwise get in the way of the file. Take this work slowly, beginning with a coarse file to remove large details and working down to a finer blade to finish off with, minimising scratches on the surface of the metal. To complete, burnish with wire wool or a wire brush on an electric drill.

Having got this far you can now begin building up the figure. I always start with the head, altering the shape of the hat as necessary, adding plumes etc, then the face with beard, moustache or sideburns, and progressing down to the collar. The torso should usually be completed next, especially if new arms are being added, and all the larger detail items at least firmly soldered or epoxied in place. Really fine detail can be left to last, minimising the danger of spoiling it at this stage. Legs come next, and should be cut and repositioned as desired, with Plastic Padding filling out any V-shaped gaps where they have been bent, and finally the new arms, where appropriate, added, together with any weapons.

When the whole figure is completed to this stage, apply a thin coat of matt grey or white paint: this will reveal any areas where your filing or filling requires further smoothing down. The matt paint should be removed when you are satisfied about the figure by immersing it in a paint remover and burnishing gently with the wire wool. Finally, the whole figure can be given an undercoat of polyurethane varnish which will seal the metal off from the air and prevent any oxidisation taking place.

Painting is such a personal thing that I won't go into it here, except to say that I always tackle the face first since this is what gives the figure most of its character, and all other painting detail should follow on accordingly. The variety of paints available for model figures is legion, ranging from the enamel colours produced by Humbrol, Airfix, Testors and Pactra to specialist ranges such as Campaign Colours, new types such as the acrylics and the old favourite of serious modellers, oils.

Three for the price of one

The three foot figures illustrated here are all based on the same model, Tradition's Old Guard Grenadier in the standing firing position. The first figure, which depicts a Chasseur à Pied of the Old Guard, is hardly a conversion at all, but is an ideal introduction to some of the basic techniques. All you need to do, in fact, is smear a little Plastic Padding over the bearskin plate and work it up to a fur-like texture to blend in with the rest of the bearskin; and cut away the cuff detail, reshaping to the pointed Chasseur-type cuffs as shown. Painting is just as for an Old Guard Grenadier, except that the plume is red over green and the epaulettes have green centres. Cuffs are red and white.

The second figure depicts a Pioneer of the Old Guard. Remove the basic figure's right arm, taking care to preserve the musket intact. Build up the beard

with Plastic Padding, and either make a new right arm as I did from Padding or choose one from another figure. The cross straps and belt are from Masking Tape, the leather apron cut from a toothpaste tube, and the axe from a piece of 10 thou plastic card on a wire handle. Note that the figure has white gauntlets covering up the cuff detail. Painting is as for an Old Guard Grenadier except that the bearskin cords are red and yellow and the tunic front is dark blue. Note the crossed axes badge worn on the right arm, red outlined yellow.

The third conversion shows a Grenadier on the retreat from Moscow. The bearskin is sawn off just above the eyebrows and the bald head built up with Plastic Padding. The musket is then cut away, the left arm bent down to clasp the bearskin, and the right arm bent across the breast in a sling made from Masking Tape. A blanket from tissue paper soaked in polystyrene cement and draped round the figure as if the wind is tugging at it completes the model. Aim for as dejected an expression as possible when painting the face!

Polish lancer 1702

This model depicts the figure shown in Blandford's *Military Uniforms of the World* and is based on the Tradition Grenadier à Cheval model. All surface detail apart from the face and boots must first be removed, including the sabre, while the bearskin must be filed down to a flat-topped cone. I next epoxied the figure to his horse to give me something larger to hold while working, and continued by building up the hat to the required height with Plastic Padding, which was then filed to shape and a plume added from Plasticine. The tunic, skirts and baggy trousers can next be built up with Plasticine, cross straps added from Masking Tape, a curved sword from plastic card and a lance from a length of piano wire. Colours are yellow under-tunic with light blue hat, over-tunic and trousers. The plume is white over red and the hat is fringed with brown fur. Straps are natural leather, boots brown and sword/scabbard black with brass fittings. The lance pennant is blue over yellow. Horse furniture I was not sure of but think it likely to have been blue and yellow also, so that is how I finished the figure.

Below *A selection of 54mm metal figures. Top row, left to right: SS machine-gunner (Jackboot); Spanish officer 1560 (Rose); and Wehrmacht Drum Major (Soldat). Centre: Pavlov Regiment drummer (Hinton Hunt) and Saxon Guard cavalry officer (Stadden). Front: Siberian Cossack 1944 (Old Guard) and Union infantryman (Strombecker).*
Right *One of the small range of Phoenix 54mm figures, this French cuirassier makes a superb action model.*

Front and rear views of Roy Dilley's two conversions from Britains hollow-cast figures described in Chapter 10. The standing figure depicts a British infantry officer of circa 1900 in full dress, resplendent in scarlet tunic with crimson sash, dark green helmet and dark blue trousers. The mounted figure is rather more involved and represents a British infantry officer wearing early First World War service dress using items from a number of Britains figures.

Above *Surely one of the most impressive model figure setpieces ever designed, the Series 77 Greek war chariot, from Cesare Milani's collection.*
Right *three Stadden (Tradition) Highlanders grouped for better effect — pipers of the 92nd (Gordons) and 93rd (Sutherland) Regiments with an officer of the 79th (Cameron) Highlanders.*

Above and left *Two of Cesare Milani's delightfully painted figures, both in 135mm scale by Cameron. They are a French Napoleonic hussar (above) and dragoon, 1810.* **Above right** *Hinchliffe 54mm kit figure depicting a trumpeter of the 2nd (North British) Dragoons in modified service dress in 1815.* **Right** *Willie (Suren) 70mm figure depicting Marshall Massena's mistress in (or out of) dragoon uniform.*

Far left *135mm scale Cameron French carabinier of 1815*. **Left** *95mm Stadden British light dragoon officer of 1812*. **Above** *Two Stadden 95mm figures from Cesare Milani's collection depicting British Life and Horse Guards officers of 1812.*

83

Above *Two magnificent Series 77 Greek warriors painted by Cesare Milani.* **Below** *This photo shows the parts included in a typical large scale metal figure kit, in this case the Ray Lamb/Hinchliffe 75mm French drummer.*

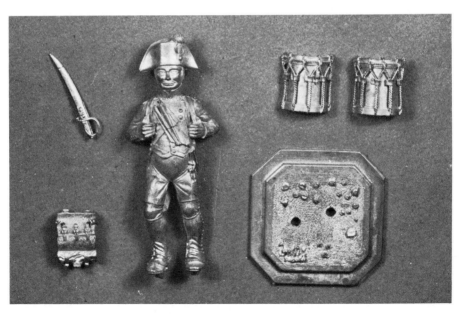

eight

Robert C. Gibson
54mm metal collectors' models

Despite the availability of hundreds of other figures in different scales, 54mm is still by far the most popular scale among figure modellers and collectors. The range of models available is so huge that even the most esoteric tastes are catered for somewhere (including the erotic!) and even if one had the time to paint a figure a day one would never exhaust all the possibilities. However, within a particular sphere—unless it is one of the extremely popular ones such as French Napoleonic or Waffen SS—the modeller aiming for a comprehensive collection may run out of commercially manufactured figures. When this happens, the only answer is to convert other suitable types to the particular model required. In this chapter, Robert Gibson explains how such conversions can be accomplished without tears, and suggests some practical examples you may care to try your hand at.

The scale of '54mm' was probably set by the prewar productions of Messrs Mignot and Britains, and it would be difficult to establish the original meaning of the term as a measurement. Today's manufacturers make collector figures to a scale which they each label as '54mm', although there are noticeable differences in relative size, often aggravated by a failure to establish the size of the historical human being on which the desired uniform is hung. Sizes vary from 54mm to 60mm when viewed comparatively, and care should be taken in collecting them lest a newly-acquired figure should look out of place alongside his apparent equals.

The makers—United Kingdom

In this section, size is given using Britains' 54mm as the standard for purposes of comparison only.

Almark (55mm) a limited range of Charles Stadden-designed figures of high quality, marketed as kits with separate arms and equipment.

Ensign (54mm) a new name but a familiar designer—Major Bob Rowe of Woburn Abbey fame. This series at present covers British Army Officers in pre-1914 Mess Dress as high quality one-piece castings, and some Napoleonic figure kits.

Garrison (55mm) produced by Greenwood & Ball, this is a limited range of inexpensive figures suitable for the beginner.

Greenwood & Ball (54mm) one of the original manufacturers, still producing their original range in painted form only. Also produces Lasset, Minot, Sanderson and Garrison figures.

Guardhouse (55mm) average quality figures in inexpensive kit form aimed at the pocket-money market. Not very original selection.

Harlech (55-60mm) two different sizes, the '1812' series being larger at 60mm than the medieval figures. Good design and moulding.

Hinchliffe (55mm) originally produced as a logical extension to their superb range of artillery (ie mounted drivers and mounted officer), the range now includes non-artillery figures, eg 1815-period British heavy cavalry, and foot figures including gun crews and 1815 period British Foot Guards. High quality figures in kit form, eclipsed only by the same firm's 75mm offerings (see Chapter 9).

Hinton Hunt (56mm) Marcus Hinton is one of the founders of the post-war industry. The range is vast and varied; the latest figures are above average quality and reasonably priced. Primer is often overdone.

Jac (55mm) nice range of unusual subjects, difficult to obtain except in the London area, and comparatively expensive.

Jackboot (54mm) as the trade name suggests, mainly German subjects. Good design but moulding quality and finish variable.

Kirk (54mm) small range of unusual subjects, mounted and foot, sold ready primed and mounted on a varnished plinth at reasonable prices. Good quality drop-cast figures.

Lasset (54mm) good range of well-designed and individually-animated figures. Lack of individual 'faces' and the pitted finish of accessories sometimes mar these high-quality products. A large range of spares is available.

Minot (54mm) rather thin but otherwise nice figures of Napoleonic hussars and soldiers of the British colonial wars and the American Indian Wars. Small range.

Phoenix (previously Les Higgins) (55mm) another small range, based largely on the English Civil War period, but with a sprinkling of other periods. The design and moulding of the newer figures is of very high quality. Mention should also be made of the excellent spares available from this manufacturer. Figures are in kit format.

Rose (54mm) Russell Gamage's beautiful figures are available in a wealth of periods from ancient Egypt to the present day. These figures are slightly more expensive than the average, and the kit format induces a lack of poses

amongst the officers. A very useful range of spare heads (with and without headwear), arms, weapons, equipment and musical instruments is available, enabling other figures to be converted.

Sentry Box (54mm) a limited range of 54mm figures is available (the firm is principally a 120mm size manufacturer) of average quality. Unusual subjects catered for (eg Sedan Chair with passenger and attendants).

Trophy (55mm) a small range of highly original subjects, some of which do not 'come off' in the metal. Quality average to good. Kit form at very reasonable prices.

Tradition/Stadden/Standish Figures (55mm) the best-known name in British 54mm size figures. A large range covering many periods. The 'Standish' kits are early Charles Stadden designs superseded by later productions, and are also supplied ready assembled and primed. Quality varies between very good and below average (in a few cases).

Valda (54mm) mainly devoted to the women's services, this range also includes some South Wales Borderers (24th Foot) of 1879, with optional colonial service and home service pattern helmets, at reasonable cost in kit format.

Not mentioned above are **Sanderson,** whose range up until the time of writing did not include model soldiers, but does include some very nice one-piece Normans in a scenic group including a blacksmith. Cliff Sanderson also designs for the Jackboot range. And **Miniature Figurines,** whose 54mm plans were not finalised at the time of writing, but who produce a handy range of 54mm swords and other equipment.

Prices for the British-made figure sold in the United Kingdom vary between 80p and £1.20 for foot figures, and £2.00 to £12.00 for mounted figures. Standard bearers, drummers and musicians are usually more expensive than ordinary soldiers at this scale, as are special animations.

Kit figures require assembly and careful undercoating (priming); theoretically assembled figures should be ready to paint, but all require filing down, and some will need repriming.

The makers—outside the UK

Few metal collector figures (other than flats) are produced in continental Europe, and the principal producers lie in Sweden and in Spain. Holger Ericsson and Soren Brunoe produce fine 54mm figures of mainly Swedish subjects (although a few 'foreigners' do creep in from time to time) and the small firm of Soldat in Barcelona produce 56mm metal figures of Wehrmacht and Waffen SS soldiers (recently marketed here under the 'Franco' label) in superb marching poses, although some of the early figures were a little slender from back-to-front.

The bulk of the non-British figures on the world markets comes from the United States of America. Most of these figures are produced in kit form, rather after the style of Rose figures, and happily, of similar quality—Valiant, Bussler, Cameo, Imrie Risley and Old Guard are all of this type. Monogram Merite produce more elaborate kits with engraved nameplate and plastic stand; Strombecker, better known for plastic products, produce one-piece lead-free castings of American Revolution, American Civil War and 1914 German subjects in boxed sets, including a 1776 cannon in the first, and a mounted officer in the second set. Vallance figures are designed by Major Bob Rowe and are largely one-piece castings in common with his other work.

This brief mention is not intended to be encyclopaedic, but covers the major commercial makers.

Tools

The average 54mm collectors' figure comes in one of three forms: either assembled and primed, assembled and unprimed, or unassembled and unprimed. Whichever form it takes, your figure will need work done on it before it can be painted. Even the assembled and primed figure invariably has moulding flash in some degree, which must be removed before painting.

A first essential, therefore, is a *sharp knife*, preferably of the exchangeable blade type, with a stout handle. Next, a good range of small *files* is useful for removing unwanted metal—round and half-round being the most useful types (a mousetail file has its uses—but restrict the use of it to light cleaning work, or it will probably snap off in a crevice that a knife-blade could have worked better).

Emery paper is invaluable for finishing, and for polishing those areas to be clear varnished as natural metal.

A *small saw* (eg jewellers' saw, or any suitable small-toothed saw) is useful for heavy cutting. One of the hobby knife manufacturers produces a razor saw for use with a heavy duty knife set, which may save expense. A *steel scribing tool* will enable you to cut lines to change the style of a coat, or add a pocket, or even improve a poorly moulded face or hand, while the use of a *hand-drill* (power drills rotate too fast for soft metals, which clog the drill bit) will enable replacement heads, etc, to be fitted with ease.

Materials

First and foremost comes adhesive or cement to fix or refix your figure in the desired position. Some of the senior practitioners of the hobby use the miniature soldering iron to fix limbs and heads, etc, in position; unless you are an expert with a soldering iron, or have time and figures to experiment with, it is not really to be recommended. Just as effective, and often more so, are the numerous quick-setting epoxy adhesives such as Devcon, Britfix 19, etc—don't use Araldite proper unless you are prepared to wait overnight for it to set, and have the means to support it while drying. The ultimate in this type of adhesive is an American product called Permabond 102, which dries in five seconds, and requires tiny quantities of glue to ensure adhesion; a British equivalent was rumoured to be on the way at the time of writing.

Also usable as an adhesive, but more commonly used to fill in moulding gaps or build up clothing is Plastic Padding. This two-tube filler is sold in two varieties, flexible and rigid and the flexible variety is most useful for model soldier work.

Thin sheet lead, obtained in the form of glue or cement tubes, is invaluable for creating belts, straps and even clothing. Brass sheet can also be purchased and is more rigid, but harder to work.

Priming

Once the metal figure is ready to paint, it is necessary to prime or undercoat it before actual painting work starts. There are many reasons for this. The early metal figures were composed entirely of lead, which suffers from deterioration from chemical action if exposed to, or insufficiently protected from, the air we breathe. Modern figures contain lesser quantities of lead—rigid figures are usually 60 per cent Fry's metal (mostly tin) and 40 per cent lead, and the more flexible figures are 40 per cent Fry's Metal and 60 per cent lead—so the old reason is still very valid.

In some cases, the paint used will not 'take' unless an undercoat of cellulose or enamel paint is applied first. Where conversion of the figure has taken place, the priming of the figure can often reveal undetected flaws prior to final painting, when they can be rectified.

The ready-assembled figure is usually ready-primed. The quality of this priming varies between manufacturers, and even between figures produced by the same maker—so you may well wish to immerse the figure in paint stripper and start from scratch. One factor that does not vary is that every manufacturer leaves untrimmed flash on the figure, whether it is primed or not, which means that it has to be reprimed after filing down.

There is a wide variety of suitable enamels and cellulose paints available for priming your figure—choose one which will give a thin overall coating, and will dry quickly. I used the 'top' of a tin of matt white enamel very successfully for years, recharging with thinners when it dried out. White is the best primer colour, since it highlights all the engraved features of the figure.

Another means of undercoating, especially useful if you do not want to spoil brushes used for water-soluble paints, is to use the cellulose primer used for car respraying work, and sold in aerosol cans. Set the figure down on its back on a large sheet of used newspaper, and spray from above employing short bursts and gentle pressure, turning the figure over and repeating the process when dry. This gives a very thin overall coating which does not obscure any fine detail. Practice will produce economic use of the aerosol.

Paints

There are three main types of paint currently available for model soldier use, namely enamels originally intended for use on plastics, oil-bound poster paints and water-soluble poster paints. The first two types require special thinners for brush cleaning and thinning; the water-soluble need plain water for thinners and a 80-20 water detergent mixture for brush cleaning.

The type of paints you choose to employ will depend on many factors, for example local supply, where you carry on your hobby, initial cost, and so on, but there are one or two guidelines in this choosing. If you habitually carry on your hobby surrounded by your family, try to avoid paints which need chemical based thinners, particularly plastic enamels, which often use a carbon tetrachloride (CTC) based mixture. This is not only unpleasant in a warm room, but it could be a serious health hazard, since carbon tetrachloride gives off a poisonous gas.

Plastic enamels often require considerable mixing before the right finish is obtained, especially where matt finishes are involved, but give a much wider range of finishes (ie matt, semi-matt and gloss) than the other types. However, the matt finish of the water-based and oil-based poster colours can be treated with matt or gloss polyurethane varnish to obtain a semi-matt or gloss finish where desirable. On the debit side, the application of clear varnish darkens the finish and tends to diminish the effect of subtle shading, so that more clearly defined shading is called for—the varnish is so thin, however, that it is possible to reshade and varnish over it again without marring the original finish.

If exact paint shades are required, it may well pay to purchase from one of the ranges of plastic enamels or oil-bound poster paints which supply these: bear in mind that you will have to mix these to provide highlighting and shading on the basic colour. The degree of accurate uniform colour information you possess will affect this: good colour guides will help you to mix your own (eg French Imperial Blue and Prussian Blue are not the same shade). I mix my own at all times, excepting the odd facing colour which matches, but even this is highlighted and shaded with mixes. Provided you are aware of the colour content of the paints you are using and the colour content of the shades you are trying to achieve, there is no need to restrict your painting to daylight hours, as some have suggested in the past. That is taking the hobby far too seriously.

Once you have decided which type of paint you will use, enlist the aid of your nearest supplier in choosing a basic range. Most suppliers will be only too glad to help you in this.

Brushes

A poor quality brush will spread loose bristles all over your work, so make sure you buy the best. Sable brushes are marketed by Winsor & Newton, Rowney and Historex Agents in the United Kingdom. They may seem expensive, but a good brush will last you for years with care. Points to remember are:

never leave paint on a brush for longer than you need it to paint with;

clean your brushes thoroughly after each spell of painting, first in thinners and then in soap and water, rinsing until the water runs clean;

if you must stipple dust colour or metal finish on figures and weapons, keep an old brush specially for this purpose—don't use your best brushes;

protect your bristles—I use hollow toothpicks as bristle covers to avoid damage to the points when not in use;

don't trim your brushes with a razor blade or by burning off the bristles—it rarely produces anything but a damaged brush, useless for any purpose.

For cleaning your brushes, household tissues are just as good as a cloth rag, and since they can be thrown away when used up, contribute to keeping your brushes and your painting clean. Avoid putting rags or tissue impregnated with plastic enamel thinners in polythene or other plastic waste bins—the CTC chemical attacks the plastic.

The basic figure

Let us assume we have a basic foot figure in kit form with a base provided, and proceed step by step through the assembly and painting processes.

First, check that the parts are all present; then check that they all fit, using a knife where necessary to remove moulding flash on joints. Once you have satisfied yourself that the kit is complete and will assemble into the desired figure, take out files, emery paper and knife and remove the moulding flash from all the parts.

Next, assemble the body (or legs, if separate) to the base by cementing in place. Place the arms, head, sword, equipment, etc on the body, and decide whether you need them separate for painting—for example, if the arms are to be extended away from the body, they would need to be painted before assembly to the body—but in other cases, difficulty may arise if the arm or pack or whatever is not painted before assembly. Use common sense to deduce whether access for the paint brush will be impeded or impaired. Where ready-assembled figures are involved, it may well pay to detach the offending part—this especially applies to hussar pelisses—and cement it back in place after painting.

Having settled in your mind how you will tackle the painting of the figure, apply the chosen undercoat to all parts, and when dry, remove the undercoat with a knife where cement or glue is to be applied. We can now proceed to the painting of the figure.

Face and hands

There are many ways of tackling the painting of a figure: I always start with the face and hands, thus giving the figure a personality from the very start. The eye sockets are given a touch of light grey, and when dry, the pupil of each eye is painted in (Fig 1). Unless you have considerable skill in wielding a paintbrush, use black only for this (observe the colour in a friend standing far enough away to be the same size as a 54mm figure, and it will be seen that only when exposed to direct sunlight do the pupils of the eyes show colour—even then it is nearly indistinguishable). Finally, edge in the upper eyelash in black, and the lower eyelash in red unless the figure is to have a very dark complexion. The face proper can now be painted.

Flesh comes in many different shades dependent on race, complexion, state of health and even local temperature conditions. For the European soldier, a basic mix of red-brown (burnt sienna) and white is suitable, and with varying amounts of yellow ochre added, will suit most Indo-Europeans and Chinese and Japanese as well. Red Indians (ie American Indians) require more red-brown in the mix, highlighting with added orange and shading with added dark brown. Most races born near the

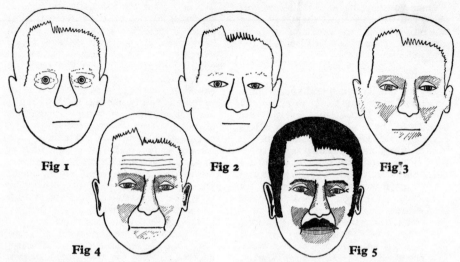

Fig 1   Fig 2   Fig 3

Fig 4   Fig 5

equator will require dark brown, high-lighted with added yellow ochre and white, and shaded with added black: the very dark Central African and South Indian races need a touch of dark blue and black added to the basic mix, high-lighting with added white and shading with added black. All the dark-skinned races have lighter skin on the soles of their feet and the palms of their hands.

Assuming that we are painting a European soldier of practically any period, a 50:50 mix of red-brown and white is prepared and applied over the whole of the face and hands, including the edges of the hair, but carefully applied around the eyes to produce a fine eyelash line (Fig 2). Now lighten part of the mix with more white paint, and apply this to the forehead, the ridge of the nose and nostrils, the eyelids, jaw, chin and the area above the upper lip. A slightly darker shade should be applied to the upper cheeks. This operation is called *highlighting*, and serves to bring out the features normally caught by light falling on the face (Fig 3).

To *shadow*, mix a shade darker than the basic finish by adding more red-brown, and apply this to the area just below the eyebrows (adding a short vertical line either side of the bridge of the nose), and in fine lines from the side of the nostrils to the corners of the mouth, across the forehead if needed, below the chin, and in the hollows and round the edge of the ears (Fig 4). A little black added to the mix will produce the usual

darkening at the inner corners of the eyes, and a little black added to the high-lighting mix will produce an unshaven effect on the chin and upper lip, ex-tending to the level of the lobes of the ears. The shadow effects described above can be produced when using water-soluble paints by thinning the 'added' colour, ie red-brown or black, to a water consistency and applying it in small amounts in the areas needed: the secret is to use only small amounts, and gradually darken to the required degree—the result is most effective. Lips are painted in with a touch of crimson in the basic mix—darker on the upper lip than on the lower.

Once the main features of the face are painted, the eyebrows, hair and any facial hair such as beards and moustaches can be painted in (Fig 5). These again can be highlighted and shadowed, especially where clumps of hair are involved, eg beards and moustaches, to bring out the shape and texture.

After the face and hair have been painted, the head can be varnished with matt polyurethane varnish to give a life-like texture. Small finishing details can be added—for example, the eyeballs can be gloss varnished, or beads of sweat can be added in gloss varnish with a fine pointed brush.

The hands have been somewhat left out, so far, but the procedure is much the same as for the face: the inner edges of the fingers are shadowed, being least lighted, the knuckles are highlighted, and veins are added to the back of the hands by adding dark blue to the basic mix. Finger tips are darker, with pinkish nails, and dirt added to taste! Where bare arms are to be painted, remember that the inside of the arm— ie that closest to the body when the arm is at rest—is paler than the outside.

Whenever you are painting 'skin', always consider the physical characteristics of the person you are portraying, and what he is doing. A fully-equipped soldier in high summer will probably be either bright pink and perspiring heavily (fair skin), or slightly perspiring and slightly more tanned than normal (dark complexion). A fair-skinned soldier in the North African desert would probably have a deep pink face, neck, hands and knees; again this is more likely with Allied rather than German troops, where the percentage of winter sportsmen was much higher and hence the chance of acquiring a deep tan before reaching the desert was greater. Again, the unhealthy conditions of trench warfare in the 1915-18 period in France produced a pale yellowish complexion amongst the 'residents' on both sides of No Man's Land. The Napoleonic soldier was more likely to have a healthy outdoor complexion than his counterpart of 50 or 100 years later, since at that time industry was in its infancy, and most people worked out of doors all their lives. As was said at the time, strong drink was 'the besetting sin of the Army' so a deeper pinkish hue on cheeks and nose is appropriate for at least some British soldiers. The foregoing comments barely scratch the surface of the subject, but if you bear in mind *who* he is, *where* he is and *what* he is doing—you will probably get it right.

Uniforms

A great many words have been spent on the man under the uniform thus far— he is very important, since at 54mm size he assumes a personality not always evident or even necessary at 20, 25 or 30mm scale, where the uniform is more important. But the larger scale provides more scope for the uniform too—piping, cockades and badges become more visible at 54mm.

Start in the deepest crannies of the uniform using the shadowing mix: paint in the shadow around belts, turnbacks, folds, coat openings, behind packs,

blanket rolls, coat tails and so on (Fig 6). Gradually lighten the colours used to 'normal' mix, working outwards 'towards the light'. Leave the painting of belts, sashes, pouches, etc, until the basic uniform is complete. The reasoning behind the 'dark into light' method is simple: when you reach the 'normal' stage, you will already have the shadow painted in and thus will be better able to judge the degree of highlighting

Fig 6

needed. Thus for an Imperial Blue coat, shadow with Navy Blue, use Imperial Blue as 'normal' and work towards Ultramarine as highlighting. Some areas such as the shoulders and the creases at the elbow will need Ultramarine, others will only need an Ultramarine/Imperial Blue mix to highlight. Try to paint the seams with a fine brush using black (or grey for light colours): this adds considerably to the realism of the garment.

It is better to leave pipings and facings until the basic colour of the garment is completely painted, unless some good reason dictates otherwise—for example, on French Napoleonic light infantry coatees where the lapels and turnbacks are of the same colour as the basic garment and are piped white, it is better to paint the piping in before the basic garment colour is applied to these areas, probably before even mixing the basic mix to ensure the same mix overall. Again, trouser stripes may be painted before the basic colour is applied. In both these cases, and in all cases concerning the painting of lines, it should be noted that it is easier to paint in the straight edges after the piping colour has been applied, since one does not have to keep 'both' edges straight at the same time, as when painting a line on to a base colour.

Buttons and badges

Buttons and badges should be painted black around the edges to give the deep shadow behind (where applicable, don't forget the button holes—a small [1mm] line going inwards from the button). Buttons and other metal ornaments should be painted with metallic enamels as far as possible, but gold or silver braiding, which is often in silk or fine wire, should be matt in finish. To achieve this, gold or silver Indian inks are an excellent medium, giving a realistic matt finish without losing brightness; brushes can be washed out in soap and water afterwards without damage.

Where large areas of bare metal such as steel or pewter exist, a good approach is to clean off the undercoat (or omit the undercoat in this area at the start) and polish with fine grade emery paper, finishing with a coat of polyurethane varnish overall. Blackened armour can be produced by a black/silver mix which can be varnished later. Care must be taken in varnishing over metallic paints: some need to dry for 24 to 48 hours beforehand (assuming they were 'mixed' correctly in the first place), others, like the water-soluble paints (eg Rose and Pelikan Plaka), can be varnished over almost immediately. If you are not sure of the performance of your paint, take it carefully.

Finishing

When the basic uniform and buttons and badges are painted in, there remains the equipment—the belts, packs, pouches, boots and headwear. Start with the belts, pouches and straps, especially where

dealing with a 'kit' figure with detachable parts: this enables the arms to be fixed in position, and the knapsack, if appropriate. Leave the headwear until last, since base and head are often the best places to hold a figure during painting. If possible, fix the figure to its intended base before painting the headwear: this gives one a firm grip outside the figure itself.

When painting the shako, helmet or other headwear, start at the bottom— paint in the shadow underneath, then work upwards leaving plumes, cockades and badges until last.

Horses

Although mounted figures in this scale are relatively expensive, and tend therefore to be a minority interest, a few words on how to paint them should not come amiss. Start to paint at the point of junction of horse and trappings, and paint in all shadows. Paint the body first after the shadows in the basic horse colour, then gradually darken to tone in all the muscles. Avoid highlighting unless you are well acquainted with horses, it is very difficult to do properly. When the body is painted, paint in the socks and blaze (on the forehead) in pale grey, and the hoofs in a dull brown (and horse shoes in steel if visible). Varnish overall (when dry) with a matt polyurethane varnish, which gives a satin finish, appropriate to all but an ungroomed horse. Paint the mane and tail in matt colour, using highlighting and shadowing; unless this is to be a meticulously-groomed horse, do not varnish. Next, paint in and varnish the harness in the appropriate colours. Finally, paint in the horse furniture, working from the undermost layers outwards, applying shadows as you go. Treat these as you would a uniform, with highlighting and shadow in the same fashion; unless you have fur saddle or holster covers, do not varnish. (See Fig 7.)

Conversions and animations

The following examples are complete in themselves, and are intended as practical examples of conversion and/or animation to give experience to those who have not tried their hand at producing a non-stock figure, and hopefully to tempt those who have. Only reasonably inexpensive figures have been used, with a minimum of accessories.

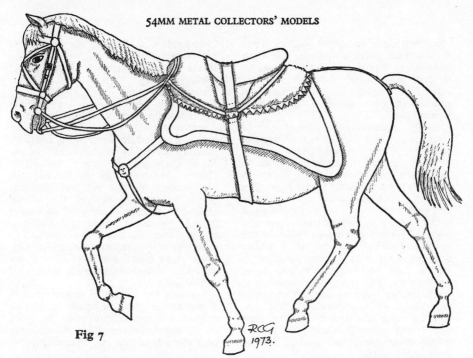

Fig 7

RCG
1973.

Conversion 1 Prussian Infantryman of the 1st Battalion, 8th Reserve Regiment, 1813.

Basis Almark 'Sentinel' Foot Guards Private, standing.

Extra parts none needed; small items for effect only.

Procedure 1—clean off the moulding flash on body and arms with knife and file, finishing with emery paper. Remove the coat of arms from the knapsack with a knife, finishing with file and emery paper (the Lasset knapsack can be used instead; check the fit at this stage). Using a saw, remove the water bottle at the left hip, then clean up the haversack beneath to remove all traces of the water bottle, using knife and file. Remove all braid from the cuffs and the front of the jacket.

2—using a suitable adhesive, cement the figure to the base. When the figure is throughly set, take right arm No 5 and the musket provided (the Lasset flintlock musket—a French Year IX pattern musket—may be used if desired), and cement the arm in position on the body so that the fingers loosely grasp the musket at or slightly below the muzzle. Do not at this stage cement the musket to the hand, but set aside until later. The figure depicted uses left arm No 4 raised slightly above the right holding a

pewter beer mug preparatory to drinking from it. As with the right arm, use the utensil grasped to fix the arm position (mark with a soft pencil on arm and body if you wish), then remove the mug and cement the arm firmly in position. The raised beer mug stance is not mandatory; the arm could equally well be placed hand on hip.

The short sword is an extra added for effect—an easily-acquired supplementary weapon discarded by a retreating French soldier, provided by a Lasset spares 'sabre-bricquet' cut up and cemented to the haversack front and rear, so as to appear to be worn underneath it.

3—at this point, undercoat the figure so far completed and the items yet to be fitted. When dry, paint overall leaving bare patches on the middle of the back and around the head above the ears for the knapsack and the cap to be fitted.

The tunic is dark blue (British dark blue), with bright green collar and cuffs and white turnbacks. All shoulder belts and straps are white or off-white, as is the haversack; the cartridge pouch is semi-matt black leather. Trousers are medium grey with dark grey gaiters and black or brown shoes beneath.

The knapsack can be painted next— black semi-matt black leather for a British-supplied pack (as kit), or brown hide with dark and light patches for a French pack (Lasset spares), and both have white straps; the rolled greatcoat is dark grey. After the paint is dry, carefully cement the knapsack into place, and add any necessary final touches with a paintbrush.

4—the characteristic peaked cap is created from the 'Belgic' shako supplied in the kit. The cords and badges are filed off, and the false front is cut down to about 2 to 3mm above the real crown. A disc of 11mm diameter is cut from thin sheet tin or lead (plastic cement tube) and cemented over the top of the altered shako to form the top of the crown, and Plastic Padding is used to build in the remainder of the crown. More filling than necessary is used, then the finished job is filed and sanded to the right proportions. The cap is then fitted onto the head, not quite square (no one wore it 'square'—it would cause acute discomfort after about five minutes that way), then painted: dark blue with a bright green band and a black leather peak (semi-matt).

5—finally the musket is painted: very dark brown wood with steel barrel and lock, and brass butt plate (brass barrel binding for French Year IX model), and cemented in position, as is the pewter mug (steel with a touch of yellow, or Plaka silver). The base is painted to taste; a black edge with yellow ochre or grass green terrain, or even railway scenic 'grass'.

Conversion 2 French Royal Guard, Dragoon officer, 1823.
Basis Standish French Line lancer officer No 45.
Extra parts none.
Procedure 1—this is a very simple conversion in terms of alterations to be done, but care is needed with the building up and finishing of the trousers. *Military Drawings and Paintings in the Royal Collection* Volume 1, by A. E. Haswell Miller and N. P. Dawnay has illustrations of the original garment (worn by lancers) and of the Guard Dragoons in grande tenue of an earlier period; Funckens' *Arms and Uniforms of All Times* Volume 2 contains colour drawings of the original uniform in 1823. Both these books are helpful, and are generally obtainable through your local public library.

2—since the kit comes unanimated in a number of parts, a small amount of animation is necessary to pose the figure on the base provided. After the flash has been cleaned off this can be attempted.

Front and rear views of the three conversions. From left to right they show the Prussian Reserve infantryman, French Royal Guard Dragoon officer and wounded Uhlan officer. In some views items of equipment described in the text have been omitted for the sake of clarity. The Uhlan officer shown here illustrates an alternative fitting for the pouch belt, and the lance cap fitted with retaining lines.

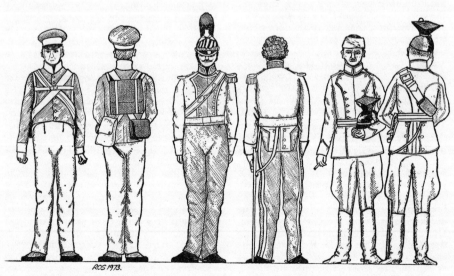

RCG 1973.

The simplest way to do this is to have the figure 'stand at ease', ie feet slightly apart (3-5mm), toes pointing outwards at not more than 35 degrees. Alternatively, the figure can be posed with the left leg bent a little at the knee and the body bent slightly forward to rest the hands on the sheathed sword for support. The leaflet accompanying the Standish kits has some useful tips on how to bend. For example, gentle bends can be managed with pliers covered in cloth or card to avoid damage to the figure. As a general rule, do not use this method for bends greater than five to ten degrees. Where a larger bend is desired, cut with a saw or sharp knife into the inside of the bend, and then carefully and slowly bend into position. Any gaps can be filled afterwards with Plastic Padding. Do not use this method to attempt bends where a pivoting movement rather than a hinging movement is required—eg movement of the upper arms or the head. This will be dealt with later in the chapter.

Try the desired position for yourself by physically attempting it—this will help to establish just how much bend is needed. With any figure, always have the hands 'busy'—don't let them just droop—for example, let one rest on the hip while the other grasps the hilt of the sword.

3—once the pose is set, cement the figure to the base and allow to set firmly. Then mix a good quantity of Flexible Plastic Padding (the blue and yellow tubes) on a tin lid or an old newspaper, and apply to the legs of the figure from groin to ankles. Do not worry about putting too much on, it can always be filed down afterwards—but too little makes more difficult. When the mixture is thoroughly dry (and not before), take a fine half-round file and file away the excess material, cleaning the file frequently and carefully with a wire brush to prevent clogging. Work at the outline first, then once that is right, use the round side to produce the deep creases spreading outwards from the knees. Constant reference to the illustrations will help you here. When you are satisfied with all your filing work, clean away the dust and fragments from the figure, then undercoat the figure and weapons ready for painting.

4—the French Royal Guard Dragoons retained much of the uniform of the 1812 Line Dragoon uniform, and the crested helmet of the restored Bourbon monarchy. The result was something like the French light-horse lancers of the Line of the 1811-15 period, except for the trousers adopted in the 1820s. The jacket was dark green, with plastron, collar, turnbacks and cuffs in crimson, trimmed in silver lace. The buttons were silver gilt; the waist sash was of silver net silk. The crimson 'Cossack' style trousers had two stripes (2mm wide in 54mm scale) down the outer seams. Boots were polished black leather. The whole outfit was topped by a black fur crested helmet of the style worn by Napoleon's French Line lancers but bearing a 'turban' of tiger skin. The sword had a gilt hilt and a black woven silk grip; the scabbard was steel with gilt fittings and silvered slings. These latter can be cut from thin sheet lead or tin, and cemented into position on the rings of the scabbard, and below the waist belt (as fitting under it) on the left hip (upper ring) and the small of the back (lower ring). Use heavy shading on the creases of the trousers to bring out the shape.

Conversion 3 Prussian Uhlan officer, 1914, wounded.
Basis Standish Prussian Uhlan officer, No 103.
Extras Rose spare head B5a—bandaged head.

The nations that went to war in 1914 employed both lance-armed cavalry and machine-guns, but the lance (and indeed all cavalry) was rendered ineffective in the face of the machine-gun. The figure depicted is of a Uhlan officer wounded in one of the murderous early encounters on the Russian front—eventually he will become part of an after-the-battle scene, contemplating a Russian Maxim machine-gun from the 'sidelines'.

Procedure 1—very little animation is employed for this figure. The legs are straightened and set 5-6mm apart with the toes ten degrees outwards from straight ahead. The left arm carries the distinctive Uhlan tschapka (lance-cap) resting on the forearm and in the crook of the elbow, and requires pulling away from the body by about 10mm (from cuff to tunic skirt), and then notched at the elbow to bend inwards at 90 degrees; the left hand is clenched. The right arm is slightly bent and hangs free, with the right hand holding a lighted cigarette (made from 22swg wire). The sword hilt rests on the back of the left forearm against the body.

2—the figure as purchased requires the complete and careful removal of the head above the collar. This is done with a sharp knife—the collar line curves, so the use of a saw could damage this—working round the collar, and gradually 'rocking' the head to obtain a deeper cut (it can be seen while doing this how one can incline the head to create a different pose in other figures). The gap left by cutting is filled with Plastic Padding afterwards.

Once the head is removed, set it aside carefully; take up the new head and shorten the peg by half its length. Drill out a hole for the new head by wrapping the body in cloth, and securing it lightly but firmly in a vice, and boring out with a drill, using a drill bit of slightly larger size than the peg diameter. Cement the new head in position after checking the fit. Finally, cement the figure to the base provided.

3—remove the cords and tassels from the left breast of the tunic with a sharp knife, being careful to leave enough metal to carve two extra buttons on the left edge of the plastron to correspond with those on the right side (and not covered by cords and tassels). Clean up using file and emery paper.

4—remove the head part from the discarded head, leaving the tschapka intact. Cut away the hanging plume, being sure not to damage the oval cockade at the edge of the crown. If in doubt, leave a little too much and complete the fining down with a file. To add a touch of realism, take a sharp point, and add a couple of bullet holes above the left ear on the tschapka, to explain the bandaged head. Undercoat both the figure and accessories, and paint when dry.

5—the tunic and breeches are field-grey in colour: 35 per cent yellow, 15 per cent black and 50 per cent white provides a good basic mix, to which add white for highlights, and yellow and black in the designated proportions for shadow (for sharp edges, ie seams, tunic edges and flaps, add black only). The inside legs of the breeches are of a chamois leather colour. Boots are tan leather, and the tschapka is black lacquered leather with a black-inside-white cockade and a brass eagle and fittings.

The figure depicted is a Leutnant (lieutenant) of the 8th Uhlan Regiment, present at Tannenburg and all the 1914 battles on the Eastern front: collar, cuffs and plastron and tunic piping is light blue. Many officers of the Prussian Uhlans are depicted in the summer of 1914 with a mixture of full dress and combat equipment: thus our Leutnant has a silver braid waist belt with two horizontal black stripes, supporting a tan leather holster for his '08 Luger pistol, and a white leather pouch belt and black leather pouch with brass fittings. The sword, gilt hilted with a grip bound in black, has a silver strap and knot with a double thread of black running through it; the scabbard is blackened steel. The sword is carried, since in the field it fitted into a frog on the equipment of the horse and not on the person.

Animation 1 Bavarian Light infantry-man, 1809-12.

Basis Standish Bavarian Grenadier private, No 80.

Extras none.

This is a straightforward animation of a standing figure, to provide a skirmisher advancing to cover, cocking his flintlock as he goes.

Procedure 1—the kit figure can be used as it comes—no parts need removal. After the moulding flash has been removed, cut notches across the upper thigh, and behind the knee of the left leg. Bend the whole leg forward, then the lower leg backward (see diagram). The foot is notched in the front of the ankle to bring it upwards, so that the figure is bearing most of its weight on its left foot. Cut a notch across the back of the right knee and bend the lower right leg backward. Bend the forepart of the right foot with round-nosed pliers. The figure is now adjusted in position so that the body is bent slightly forwards, bearing most of the weight on the left foot, with the right foot to the rear (ie advancing at a trot rather than a run).

2—the arms are now positioned: the left arm is notched inside the elbow, so that it bends upwards and forwards across the body to hold the musket half-way down the barrel. The right arm is more gently bent forwards to place the right hand over the hammer of the flint-lock—the hand being eased into a clenching-and-cocking action with round-nosed pliers. Use the musket to set up the positions of arms and hands—then remove it.

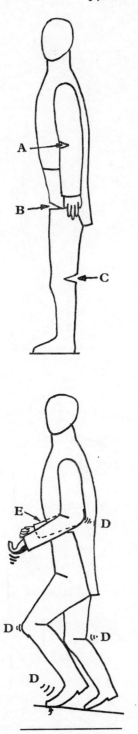

3—when the figure is animated to your satisfaction, cement it to the base, and let it set. When dry, undercoat the figure and the weapons and allow to dry. Do not add the weapons until after painting.

4—after painting the face and hands, proceed to the coatee which is a dark green in colour. Facing colours—on collar and cuffs only—are red, yellow or black, according to regiment, further distinction being added to cater for six regiments by the use of brass or pewter buttons. Lapels (plastron), cuff patches, shoulder straps and turnbacks are dark green, piped in red, as are the collar and cuffs. Breeches are medium grey, and gaiters and boots black. The black lacquered leather helmet has a black furred-wool crest, with a brass badge and fittings, and the light infantry plume on the left side is dark green.

Belts are white: the cartridge pouch is black, and the bayonet and sword scabbards are brown leather with steel bayonet and brass sword hilt (some contemporary prints omit the bayonet). The knapsack is brown untanned hide with white fastening straps, and the rolled greatcoat medium grey with white retaining straps. The musket is dark brown wood with steel barrel and fittings with a white sling.

Animation 2 Private, Hardenburg's Regiment, loading musket (Hanoverian Army, 1782).

Basis Standish British Line infantryman, Battalion Company, 1777 (No 98).

Extras none needed, but Almark's Brown Bess used in original.

Although a very sound 'standard' figure, the need was felt to do something different—hence the Hanoverian defender of Gibraltar—but the same animated figure can be painted in the intended uniform. The animation is fairly complex, providing a variation from the eternal firing and standing still poses.

Procedure 1—the legs require little animation on this occasion, other than spreading 10-12mm apart, feet outwards at ten degrees from normal and knees slightly bent.

2—the right arm is cut from the body at the shoulder seam, and set aside. The

Simplified diagram showing animation 1. **A** *cut (both arms).* **B** *cut (left leg).* **C** *cut (both legs).* **D** *bend.* **E** *right arm. Note forward tilt of figure.*

left arm is notched and bent upwards and forward to grasp the musket at mid point, the butt at the inside of the left foot and the muzzle 5mm in front of the right shoulder seam.

3—the action of raising the right arm to above shoulder level, at which position the termination of the ramming home action occurs, shortens the shoulder-to-elbow distance by a small amount. The arm is therefore cut as shown in the diagram, and notched to bend the fore-arm back sharply at 30 degrees to the upper arm. This position is checked carefully, using the musket, before the right arm is reaffixed to the body. After the arm is set, build up the gap left with Plastic Padding, allowing extra for the pull on the material of the coat produced by the raising of the arm. After thorough drying, cut and file away the excess, then clean off all dust and filings, and finally undercoat the figure and accessories ready for painting.

4—first paint the face and hands: the use of a moustache is almost obligatory for a Hanoverian soldier (those who could not grow moustaches in Continental armies were obliged to 'paint' one on in black charcoal or similar medium). The hair is powdered and tied with a black ribbon at the nape of the neck. A white collarless shirt is worn with a black leather stock round the neck, then a white waistcoat with pewter buttons, and finally on top of this a madder red coat with black facings—ie cuffs, lapels and turnbacks—and square white button lace on cuffs and lapels and on the tail pockets—one line of lace per button. As on the waistcoat, pewter buttons. Breeches are chamois leather colour, and gaiters and boots black. The black tricorne hat has a white edging and a black silk ribbon cockade. All belts are white, and the bayonet is steel. White shirt cuffs are partly visible under the coat cuffs.

The musket is dark brown wood with a 'browned' steel barrel and fittings (soon removed by excessive polishing for parades) and a brass butt plate. The ramrod end is detached carefully and reaffixed in the muzzle itself: this item is also steel.

Simplified diagram showing animation 2.
A *cut along this line.* **B** *remove.* **C** *cut notch.* **D** *bend.* **E** *fill with Plastic Padding after arm is reset.* **F** *gentle bend across body.* **G** *legs apart.*

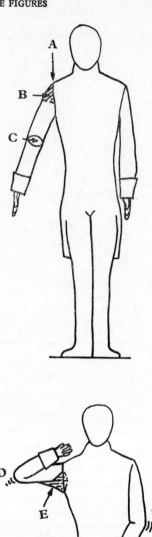

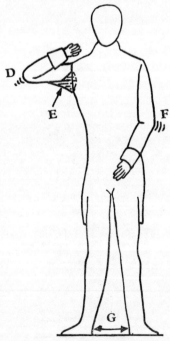

nine

Cesare Milani
Large-scale metal figures

The author of this chapter is well known for his excellent figure modelling articles in Military Modelling *and needs no further introduction here. In the following pages he reviews the various ranges of larger scale metal figures currently available, and shows how he tackles the problems of painting and animation. These larger figures tend to be very expensive, but they really do lend themselves to careful painting and the finished results in many cases would do credit to a museum. They also have the inherent advantage of being less 'fiddly' to paint if your skills do not run to painting pupils in the eyes of 20mm soldiers. Because of their size and price, actual conversion work is usually impractical, though if you wanted to try it the same techniques as outlined by Robert Gibson in the previous chapter could equally well be used on 75, 77, 90 or even 120mm models.*

It must seem rather obvious that the bigger a figure is, the better its smaller parts can be reproduced and the minute details rendered with greater accuracy. Unfortunately this is not always the case, and, inexplicably, in many of the figures that I have examined, the bigger the size, the less accurate the detail. Of course there are exceptions. There are some absolutely splendid large figures, but these are normally unique pieces and do not belong to a commercial series which is what we are discussing now. To my mind the ideal size should not exceed 100mm. Too big a figure can loose the subtle charm of the miniature.

I started my modelling with the standard 54mm plastic figures. To be precise, with Historex figures of incomparable beauty and their unbelievable reproduction of the finest detail. As I like to transform and animate figures, making little groups, copying from old paintings and the like, and my skill with metal work is rather modest, I preferred to stick to the plastic figures leaving the metal ones alone, beautiful though they may be. I was afraid of being restricted in my creative expression.

Then one day I saw a figure much bigger than the standard size, metal, made by '77 Series'. It was an 1810 French Mounted Hussar so striking that I decided that, metal or no metal, it was something that I *had* to try and paint. Animation with figures of that kind could come later. I was not disappointed. The technique acquired in painting the 54mm figures had been a great help, particularly in the smaller areas. However, I found that painting a larger figure requires a different approach.

Masses and volumes are larger and depressions deeper. As the contrast between light and shadow is less relevant, a more subtle and softer brushwork is required. Mind you, the way of painting a figure can change drastically from one to another. Compare, for instance, the beautiful body of a Greek warrior (Series 77), practically naked and splendidly modelled, whose features are reminiscent of a classic sculpture; and the martial aspect of, say, a hussar officer in parade dress. The play of the muscles and the texture of the skin of the Greek warrior require subdued tints and delicate blending, whereas the material of a garishly coloured uniform, the leather of the boots, the shine of metal buttons, epaulettes and all the accoutrements (plenty of them in a hussar's uniform) offering a much greater contrast, need more panache in the rendering of tones. What I found vital is that one should try to create a dynamic, life-like look. So many figures that could be beautiful are spoilt by a static appearance through too heavily shadowed dresses and doll-like faces.

The stance and gestures of a figure speak for themselves, but if the facial expression does not reflect them the result is dull and lifeless. To give a particular expression to a sculptured face is, of course, easier said than done, but with a little practice and patience one can change that face to suit a particular mood. I often change the shape of a nose, for instance, just because I don't like it or because it seems to me that it does not fit the character of the person represented. For this simple operation I find Plasticine very useful. With it one can also alter the cut of the eyes and the shape of the cheek bones, so enabling one to change the figure to a different race or period.

Of all the expressions one can give a face I have found a laughing one the most difficult. The eyes narrow, cheeks rise, chin recedes, and wrinkles form around the mouth, not to talk of the teeth, which generally have to be made, in full view. But that can be managed quite all right with attentive observation in front of the mirror, hoping that nobody comes into the room and thinks that you have gone round the bend.

A help when painting a figure is a reference to contemporary paintings on which to check the correct colours of uniforms and the expression and tone of the faces. Plasticine, as I said before, is a good medium for this kind of transformation. It sticks well to the metal and once painted over with an undercoat it acquires enough strength to withstand the usual painting. Of course, one must not handle the figure where the Plasticine was put on, at least for a long setting period, but that is obvious. Figures of this size are not for wargames and once on their display position they stay put.

Talking of minor alterations, often the figure requires attention to the hands. They may be clumsy, due possibly to casting problems, and require small modifications either to reflect a particular mood or to enhance a given expression. One has to bear in mind that hands are as important as faces, and leaving them as they come can spoil the whole figure. Cutting through metal to separate the fingers is not an easy job. In any case not as easy as with plastic, but epoxy resin can work miracles and restore a finger chopped off and set it in a new position.

Epoxy resin has opened new horizons in my struggle with animation in metal. The soldering iron can be very tricky. Some parts of a figure require a good deal of heat for soldering, and some others can be melted away in no time. So when I started using epoxy, I was more or less back to the technique I use with plastic and in spite of the different material I was able to achieve some fairly decent results. All depends, of course, on what the modeller wants to do with his figures. Some collect and paint them just for the uniform and some prefer to have a live scene, as in a diorama.

As recently released figures have plenty of built-in animation, in many cases alterations are not necessary, so it is just a matter of painting. When I start, the first thing I do is to get rid of the flaws in the casting. Some have less than others, but generally a thorough cleaning-up job is necessary for all of them. Some figures come in kit form and so it is necessary to see that all the parts fit neatly. I find Polyfilla a good material to fill up gaps. The alterations to the figure then follows, either animation or minute changes to faces and hands. Before starting painting a good wash is very important (detergent or even lemon juice are rather good), followed by an undercoat of matt white which brings up the fine details. Better several thin coats than one thick one.

Up to now I have talked about human figures, but one must not forget the horses! Series 77 produce some fine horses whose castings require very little

The first mounted figure ever manufactured by Series 77 was this French hussar of 1810. He is dressed in the uniform of the élite squadron of the 11th Hussars.

The adversaries. Both of these figures are to 90mm scale by Stadden. That on the left is a French Old Guard grenadier in full dress, that on the right a Black Watch officer of 1810.

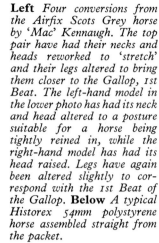

Left *Four conversions from the Airfix Scots Grey horse by 'Mac' Kennaugh. The top pair have had their necks and heads reworked to 'stretch' and their legs altered to bring them closer to the Gallop, 1st Beat. The left-hand model in the lower photo has had its neck and head altered to a posture suitable for a horse being tightly reined in, while the right-hand model has had its head raised. Legs have again been altered slightly to correspond with the 1st Beat of the Gallop.* **Below** *A typical Historex 54mm polystyrene horse assembled straight from the packet.*

Three complicated horse conversions by 'Mac' Kennaugh. The top model depicts a wounded horse struggling to rise and is based on the Airfix Hussar horse. Body and head, are assembled first, then the rear quarters cut off just forward of the hip, rear legs separated and repositioned as shown. The body is then cut into three — forepart and two mid-body sections — and the whole rearranged 'by eye' to give the right effect, with a slight leftward twist to the whole body and neck. The centre model representing a falling horse was made in virtually the same way, adapting the cuts to the new position required. To simplify matters, front legs from the Scots Grey horse were incorporated. The remainder of the 'Grey horse forms the basis for the bottom conversion, this time using ex-Hussar horse front legs — a good example of economic cross-kitting.

Three more of 'Mac' Kennaugh's horse conversions. **Top** *A basic Airfix Scots Grey horse on right with a modified one illustrating the 1st Beat in the Gallop on the left.* **Centre** *A Hussar horse converted to the correct position for the 3rd Beat of the Walk when the right foreleg is being brought forward to be placed on the ground. The head and neck have also been 'drooped' as for a tired animal.* **Left** *Airfix Scots Grey horse on the left converted to the 2nd Beat of the Gallop with head and neck stretched forward. The model on the right is the Hussar horse in a later stage of the 2nd Beat and is leading right, while that on the left is leading left.*

work, However, since the rider is generally soldered to his horse, one must try to get them separated because otherwise, when painting, the figure is very difficult to handle on account of the weight, and the details of the saddle and rider's legs are at disadvantage. Separating the rider from his mount with a soldering iron requires great care so as not to spoil the details, but small damage can be repaired and, also, a really tight fit on the saddle can later be obtained. There is nothing worse than seeing a rider sitting on thin air.

In autumn 1973 Hinchliffe Models presented the first three figures in a new 75mm series modelled by Ray Lamb. Knowing Ray and his artistic approach in painting figures, I was not surprised to see that his sculpting was also good, and so different in style from all other metal figures. The series started with a French infantry drummer, Napoleonic period, which had such character and such superb fine detail as to make it really outstanding. With his little protruding tummy and a funny face full of humour, the figure was a joy to paint. Other figures followed, all of the same period and all of the French infantry of the Line. The castings are virtually faultless and the detail extremely accurate, crisp and highly defined. I particularly like a grenadier holding his musket as in a hand-to-hand fight. His hooked nose (which this time I did not dare change) and his heavily hooded eyes make him a perfect 'Grognard', the old grumbler hardened in a hundred battles. His hands, grabbing the weapon, are stupendous (no need here for modifications) and very expressive in the tenseness and strength they show. The series, which is continually growing, at the present moment is all of the French Napoleonic period but I am looking forward to the British and to some mounted figures.

Ray has already made one very distinctive figure, the now famous Japanese Samurai in a much bigger scale. This is a unique figure with a terrific stance and fantastically detailed armour. It has been illustrated in many reviews (especially in *Military Modelling*) so there is no need to go into details here. It is really outstanding in size and beauty. Here again a different technique is required, and since there are many colour pictures of it published in various magazines, one just has to try and imitate Ray's technique. I did but the result left a lot to be desired, to say the least!

77mm, not surprisingly, is the size of Series 77 figures, though actually the real size varies slightly from figure to figure. The series, created by Pat Bird, started with two figures: one on foot, one mounted, both French Napoleonic. Since then it has grown incredibly with literally dozens of figures divided in different 'Stages' that cover periods of history from ancient Greece up to today. If one compares the very first figures to the latest ones, one can see a definite improvement not only in the casting but also in the already good modelling. The figures show more character, better animation and the small parts of the accoutrements are modelled with terrific detail and accuracy.

I like the horses because they are not beautiful. It seems absurd, but their horses are a representation of animals of no particular breed, horses that could have been picked up after a battle, requisitioned from peasants, anything but horse-show animals as often represented in other makes. These horses are down to earth and real. Unfortunately the head has the harness modelled on and in some particular cases that has to be modified, but that does not require any particular skill. Just erase with a file and make a new one in plastic card. The bits are a little crude and have generally to be remade, being a very important part of the horse head. They could otherwise spoil a beautiful figure.

Among the many figures produced by '77' there are some outstanding ones that have a favourite place in my collection. One is a lancer which I painted with the Vistula Regiment colours, charging on his horse, which is a particularly well modelled animal. Another is a Greek warrior, coming home and carrying his little boy on his shoulders: a little scene full of human warmth. There are many others, of course, and particularly two mounted knights in armour of AD 1500. The horses also wear armour, which is splendid and very finely chiselled. With these figures, as with all others wearing steel armour, there is not much to paint, but the representation of the metal requires particular care. I did mine by first getting rid of the undercoat paint in which the figures are supplied. Then, with very fine steel wool, I worked the bare metal till it shone. Rubbing compound and finally a metal polish produced the required brilliant surface. After that I covered the lot with a mixture of black and Prussian blue. When dry, I rubbed it down lightly so as to leave the paint only in the depressions. Clear varnish then covered everything. The result was good and I can recommend this technique.

Recently Series 77 produced some rather unusual new items, for example a coat of arms of 1560 displayed on a stand as armour was kept when not in use (they did not keep it folded in a drawer with mothballs), and to go with it a couple of swords, a set of polearms, a musket and a rather elaborate crossbow with quiver and bolts. Very good casting and plenty of detail. The scale is 120mm. In the same scale there are also two busts on a plinth, one of Napoleon and the other of a Saxon Guard officer of 1900. This particular 'Stage' stands apart from the other 77mm 'Stages' which cover a wide variety of times and different uniforms and nationalities. 77mm is almost an ideal size for a figure, since it is small enough to allow one to build dioramas of a fair size.

In a slightly bigger scale, 95mm, there is a splendid series of figures created by Charles Stadden. They are all on foot, including cavalry troops and, as can be expected, very well sculptured, starting with British and French troops of the Napoleonic period and running up to the present day with a figure of a Coldstream Guard on sentry duty, complete with FN Rifle. The French Army is headed by a beautiful model of Bonaparte which represents him as he was at Waterloo, clad in his characteristic long grey coat, and rather plump. The ever popular grenadier of the Imperial Guard is a splendid figure which goes well alongside a trumpeter of the Empress Dragoon Regiment in a resplendent uniform. Wellington at Waterloo, cocked hat in his hand, is the most representative figure of the British Army if not the most colourful. For that there are plenty of other figures to show the glitter of gold and steel, the blue and the scarlet of the Guards, the green of the Rifle Brigade and the different, all glamorous, colours of the uniforms of the Indian Army.

I have a few favourites in this series

and particularly an Officer of the Guards 1815. As the uniform of the Life Guards and the Horse Guards differs only in the colour of the tunic and the plume, I got two figures and painted accordingly, altering slightly the manner in which each figure holds his sabre. The two Regiments *had* to be represented! There is also a figure of a contemporary trooper of the Guards which I also duplicated to represent Life and Horse Guard. On their cuirasses I tried a different technique. As the metal was rather porous I painted it with several coats of matt white, rubbed down in between until the surface was absolutely smooth. That was coated with Japan Gold Size, on which, when tacky, I applied with great care silver leaf of the kind used for gilding frames etc. This, when absolutely firm, that is to say after a few days, was burnished and acquired a splendid shine. This process was rather laborious because I had to start again several times after accidentally ripping some of the silver leaf in the process of burnishing. To be honest I would not recommend it, but it was a challenge and one has to experiment.

There are many figures in this series and all very good, especially the stance and the well modelled faces. The castings need some work and in all cases the spurs need to be remade. For that I use fuse wire and a little wheel (any old watches at hand?). No painting instructions come with the figures and the modeller has to check with his reference books for the details, but since all the figures are of well-known regiments this is no difficulty. The series is continually gaining new figures, all very interesting and well modelled.

In a very similar size, another range of excellent figures has recently been released. The series, called 'Men o' War' has been created by Miss Sandoe, whose masterful hands blend a delicate feminine touch with strong, vigorous modelling. The very first figures, of Napoleonic Polish lancers and a musketeer of the English Civil War period, had an immediate impact, especially on people like me who do not buy a figure just for the uniform but look for some form of art and beauty. The very latest at the time of writing was a drummer of the French Army 1915, showing him sitting on the ground writing a letter home, using his drum as a 'desk'. His expression, the position of his hands, the way he is sitting among all his paraphernalia, adds up to a very artistic figure, very human and warm.

From a much bigger series, Cameron 135mm, I got three figures: an hussar, a dragoon and a carabinier of the French Imperial Army around 1810. Good stance and well modelled features, but one would have expected the smallest parts of the accoutrements and weapons to be more finely reproduced. It took a lot of work to improve the shape of the hands, sabres and musket. The plumes, rather clumsy, had to be treated with a carving tool and hot iron to give them a feathery look. All in all these figures are a bit too big to my taste and as the result was not as good as I expected from the castings (certainly my own fault) I did not continue to collect the series.

I also had a bitter disappointment with an even bigger figure of a mounted British hussar. I had better not mention the make! It comes in kit form, horse and rider in several pieces which were so desperately ill fitting that in spite of succeeding, with a lot of work, in putting the figure together, I gave up after having painted the horse and discovering how out of proportion his neck was.

A very amusing set of eight figures created by Edward Suren of 30mm fame represents various uniforms of the Napoleonic period, worn, in a matter of speaking, by some beautiful ladies. Starting with the well-known mistress of Marechal Masséna in a rather undressed state wearing the dragoon uniform, they all are showing some parts of their bodies, the best parts I should say, under rather disarranged uniforms. They are beautifully modelled and the detail not only of the physique but of the uniforms is wonderfully represented. These figures are fun, not at all out of place, especially in our permissive times. They are beautiful and a challenge to the modeller in painting not only the uniform but also in reproducing the warm silky texture of the soft feminine skin. For this I used a mixture of matt white enamel with oil Burnt Sienna and a hint of green. After blending the dark and light tones in the finest possible way I went all over the skin with a very thin coat of oil Flesh Tint. This gives life to the texture and smooths down any possible too high contrast. The bright colours of the uniform with all the trimmings then contrast sharply against the delicate tint of the skin and the result is rather appealing. Sex appealing, what? This is a self contained series which with its rather humorous charm reflects a less known aspect of the hard times armies on campaign had to endure . . .

As I am not making a comparison between smaller and bigger figures I am not going to analyse the pros and cons of both sizes. The bigger metal figures, however, offer a problem. There are so many new releases coming out incessantly that one cannot keep up with them. I have boxes full of unpainted figures which I liked so much in the bare metal state that I *had* to purchase them. Then everyday life, business and a lot of other things curtail the time to dedicate to the hobby and there they are, waiting patiently to come to life under the masterful strokes of my paintbrush! Little do they know that it is not as artistic as they deserve . . .

Another problem is how and where to display them. The figures, to be seen at their best, cannot be put too near to each other and should be observed possibly from various angles. A mirror at the back of the display cabinet can help but one must be careful in positioning it. It must be slightly tilted so you do not see yourself reflected in it. Display cabinets must be dustproof and possibly illuminated on the inside. A good solution I find is to use some discarded picture frames, bought for more or less nothing, behind which I build a box. The frame is hinged on it and a strip of plastic foam stuck all around makes it dustproof. For the shelves I use plain glass so that the light, situated at the top of the box just behind the frame and invisible from outside, can reach every part of it. Four or five shelves, depending on the size of the figures and the frame, can produce a very good display.

As I mentioned before, figures very large in comparison to the standard 54mm size are not the ideal for a collection but, of course, they can stand separately and be beautiful on their own. To my idea, though, they belong more to the 'objets d'art' than to the military figures class. I certainly did try my hand on some rather large figures, including horses, but I found that painting them was rather uninteresting and in the end just boring. Too little challenge where there is no need to bring up the details which in the smaller figures are so minute that without the help of painting they would be more or less invisible. What is fascinating, and that goes for all classes of figures big or small, is the research prior to the actual work of putting the figure together and painting. Most of them come with an instruction sheet or colouring chart, and in some cases, like Historex, with a brief historical note. But in some other cases there is just a mention of a Corps or nothing at all. This is the moment to begin browsing in the books and magazines to find the appropriate illustration of that particular figure. Even if I know the Regiment, the year etc, I always try to find out something more about the figure, some details of its uniform that are not well enough described or illustrated and, mostly, about the environment of that particular unit and period. As I have no filing system and am rather untidy with my books I often spend hours trying to find an illustration or an article that I remember having seen somewhere in some publication! I have a nearly complete collection of *Tradition* and the state of these splendid magazines certainly shows the use they have been put to.

It is a fact that a modeller of military figures is bound to try and get more information than he gets from the little boxes he takes home from the shop. And that's how one, without realising it, builds up a real reference library. Then there are people like me who want to know more and more not only about the uniforms but also about the life, the customs, and about the events and motives that generated them. In brief all about the history of that time. It is not too late to realise that the lazy hours spent in studying history, when at school, did not make a great impression and that almost all is forgotten. It is this rediscovery of lives, personalities and events that gives an ever new impulse to add figures to one's collection, not for the figure itself, but for what it represents. Why does one make groups and dioramas, not necessarily representing a combat but sometimes a more idyllic mood, if not to bring back a particular moment in life. That is the romantic background that known or unknown is the real driving force behind the modeller of military figures.

ten

Roy Dilley
Old Britains' figures

As I said at the beginning of this section, Britains were the first manufacturers of round figures to a standard scale. Although their products are now all of plastic, sufficient numbers of the older, hollow-cast metal models still exist to enable a collection to be assembled. In particular, if you enjoy conversion work, the more battered pieces can still be obtained at very reasonable prices, and as Roy Dilley shows here can be turned into very attractive models which compare favourably with the 'modern' makes. The fact that the figures are hollow confers both advantages and disadvantages, and Roy also shows how to take advantage of the former and overcome the latter.

Enthusiasts who undertake the conversion of the charming miniature metal figures which were manufactured by Britains Ltd from the 1890s until barely a decade ago, with only a brief break in production during and shortly after the Second World War, must accept the fact that the raw material with which they work is simultaneously becoming scarcer and more costly. They will therefore fall into two main categories, those who utilise damaged or incomplete items, and those who are prepared to alter pieces that would otherwise remain whole and in their original paintwork. Of recent years, original Britains' metal items in good condition have increased steadily in value, and some high prices, often outstandingly so, are realised at sales and auctions for the rarer or more spectacular sets. Even common or garden sets are in increasing demand among dealers and collectors, some of whom are concerned to a greater degree with the investment potential than with the models themselves.

However, of the millions of pieces produced over something in the order of 70 years, fair, albeit decreasing, numbers still exist, and of these a proportion, whilst complete as to the actual castings, have paintwork that has become chipped, faded, or has otherwise deteriorated, and, in consequence, are not in the condition required to command the best prices and investment possibilities. With models such as these, and with the broken or incomplete items previously mentioned, the converter can practice his art without undue expense.

What then is meant by the term 'conversion'? It implies the alteration and adaptation of 'standard' models into different attitudes, orders of dress, or types, which could not be represented merely by repainting. Conversion can be carried out entirely on the component parts of one figure, or pieces taken from two or more can be united in the creation of a completely separate item. Thus, for instance, a marching infantryman can be converted into a charging one by re-animation of the limbs, head, and torso, without necessarily changing its identity, whilst an entirely different type can be created by changing some of its parts with those from another figure or figures.

Obviously the opportunities offered by conversion for change, addition, and variety in a collection, are limited only by the material available, and by the skill and imagination of the converter. Gaps left by the manufacturers in various groups can be filled, and inaccuracies corrected; vivacity can be instilled into the more stilted attitudes; and pieces of real artistic and practical value can be produced. My own collection contains a large number of converted figures, mostly from Britains' models, whose hollow-cast construction and lead-alloy composition lend themselves particularly well to the process. Other factors making Britains' ranges eminently suitable for conversion are the generally high standard of anatomical proportion, the extremely wide variety of dress and equipment portrayed, the multiplicity of attitudes of men and animals, and the reasonably close adherence to scale within a particular range.

The overwhelming majority of Britains were turned out in 'Standard' scale, that is 1:32, 54mm or 0 Railway Gauge, and the scale was so well maintained that parts from almost any one of the hundreds of basic figure designs are compatible with those from all the others. This circumstance makes the task of the converter less difficult than it might otherwise have been, and the overall high quality of modelling allows even a beginner to achieve creditable results. Although designed as commercial items, to be produced in huge quantities for the toy trade, Britains incorporate a level of accuracy and proportion that makes it possible for conversions to be carried out on them which will result in pieces comparable in most respects to the 'connoisseur' figures currently on the market.

For really effective conversion of metal items, one needs to have mastered the skills involved in the arts of soldering, proper management of tools, and/or the use of modern adhesives of the epoxy and acrylate types. Then, too, an eye for the best figures or components which can be made to combine in the most harmonious ways is of the greatest value, together with a basic knowledge of anatomical proportions, balance, and the ways in which the limbs of men and animals move. Above all, the imagination to combine skills, judgment and knowledge in the creation of convincing and vivacious miniatures is the hallmark of the successful converter.

Advice and instruction from established modellers, plus plenty of practice, will enable a beginner to gain competance in the use of tools and materials, and to develop his own skills and techniques. Knowledge of all kinds relevant to dress, equipment, anatomy, and the general background to tactics and campaigns, can readily be acquired from the great number of books and prints which can nowadays be had at reasonable cost, or be borrowed from public libraries. Flair and imagination can, however, neither be taught nor learned from books, but may be stimulated and developed by the enthusiasm with which a subject or situation is approached, and will without doubt be enabled to operate with greater scope, the more they are backed up with accurate information and practical ability. Therefore get to know the models that you have available for conversion, break them down in your mind's eye into their component parts so that you have a sound idea of your basic material for any given pose, and practice with your tools on all the substances that you intend to use in your work, to familiarise yourself with as wide as possible a range of skills. Draw on the knowledge you have accumulated from the study of reference data for precision in the representation of attitude, costume, and impedimenta, and, most importantly, give your imagination rein so that the end result can be visualised before the actual work of conversion is commenced.

Tools required in the conversion of hollow-cast metal figures are relatively few and inexpensive, and you will be able to carry out even the most elaborate work with just the following: a small soldering iron together with good quality solder; a piercing or jewellers' saw with fine tooth metal-cutting blades; a selection of files of the 'needle' or 'warding' variety; and a scribing or cutting tool. Engravers with different gouging and cutting edge sections are extremely useful (but not essential) additions, though they do tend to be a little costly. Good work can be done with discarded dental instruments, (so keep a friendly relationship with your dentist!), which being made from high quality steel, take and retain a keen edge even under conditions of severe usage. Small pliers, and a miniature vice are all that are necessary to complete a tool kit that will be adequate for all eventualities. Useful materials are brass and copper shim and wire, pins of varying lengths, and metal foils whether of lead or aluminium base. The adhesives I have already mentioned, that is epoxies, such as Devcon and Araldite, or acrylates, like IS12, are also invaluable, and can cut out a great deal of soldering and subsequent cleaning up. It is advisable, when solder and adhesives are to be used in the construction of the same model, to carry out, where possible, the soldering operations first so as to minimise any heat damage to adhesive-bonded areas.

Now for the actual figures themselves, whether entire or incomplete in some respect. The metal must be clean and bright before bonding of either type, solder or adhesive, can be fully effective, so all paint, grease and dirt must be removed thoroughly. This can be done by boiling in a strong solution of sugar-soap, such as that marketed by Mangers, rinsing in clean water, then ensuring that all surfaces inside and out are completely dry before brushing all over with a stiff bristled brush. In order to seal the blow-hole, characteristic of hollow-cast figures, and thus prevent the ingress of solution during the boiling process, scrape off the paint around the hole to leave bright metal, then close it with a dab of solder. Failure to do this will result in a figure that will leak an unpleasant liquid over your work, tools and bench as soon as you start to cut into it for major conversion purposes, or that will, in cases where the main cavity is unpierced, subsequently be attacked by an eruption of a corrosive crystalline mass from the blow-hole, a phenomenon that will usually strike only after painstaking and time consuming painting has been completed! It is also possible to remove paint by immersing the item, after sealing the blow-hole, in a paint-stripper, cellulose thinners, or similar, then rinsing and

brushing as for the previous method. It should be noted that some of the earlier Britains' pieces were cast from an alloy having a higher lead content than that used in later years, and in consequence have a darker appearance even when cleaned and brushed.

Having decided upon the result that you wish to obtain, and with your materials cleaned up and absolutely dry, proceed to the actual cutting and joining together of the various parts. Cuts should be made as fine and accurate as is consistent with the pieces available, and care exercised to avoid breakage or distortion of delicate sections, since hollow-cast figures do not necessarily have shells of consistent thickness throughout. Then having, where relevant or feasible, carried out a dry run, assemble the parts together to make up the new figure or alteration. It is best, I have found, to build up the body of the man or animal first, before adding any separate items of armament and equipment, as in this way these latter items can be made to fit or hang in the correct positions in relation to the attitude of the piece. Another good rule is to fit the head as the ultimate stage in the figure assembly, drilling out the collar cavity where necessary, and building up a neck spigot on the head, which when fitted to the collar enables it to be adjusted to whatever position is desired, and be held firmly whilst being secured permanently in place. The traditional matchstick serves as a very efficient spigot in cases where a head is being bonded to the trunk with an adhesive.

When joining parts with solder, remember that a sufficiency of heat is the secret of success, because the molten solder must actually fuse with the base metal of the portions to be joined to create an effective and reliable union. Keep in mind also the fact that heat will flow from the point of the iron towards the coolest sections of these items, usually those with the greatest mass, so that some pre-heating of large parts may be necessary. This may be accomplished under a grill, turned fairly low (for the melting point of the piece must not be reached!), or in an improvised oven, a tin box over a candle flame, spirit-lamp, electric iron element, or other suitable source of heat. Only experience, gained by trial and error, will indicate just how long pieces should be heated under the particular method that you adopt, but, although it may seem to involve a certain amount of trouble, this pre-heating process is well worthwhile in terms of successfully soldered joints, and the prevention of much exasperation and irremediable damage to delicate detail or castings. I also find it preferable to clean up each soldered joint as it is made, thus keeping the model as clean-cut as possible while it is being assembled, and reducing the possibility of harming fine moulding that might be caused by large amounts of cutting, paring, and filing when the figure is in a fully made up condition, especially where some joins might be in places difficult to reach for these purposes.

Make sure that the attitudes you cause your models to assume are in accordance with anatomical fact and balance, and are consistent with the activity and setting you are depicting. Few men, for instance, could be found who could sprint across deep mud or snow whilst carrying a 3-inch mortar barrel! This is the area in which your knowledge of basic anatomy and observation of reference data, photographs and prints will be of immense importance, and will prevent you from producing models that fail to convince by reason of attitudes that are impossible under real life conditions of anatomy, burden, costume or environment.

Where bonding is to be effected by means of adhesives, use the minimum amount compatible with a secure join, and avoid getting any surplus over surrounding areas, since it will only have to be cleaned off again, with the consequent risk of damage to the casting. Some sort of aid in keeping parts to be secured in contact during the setting-time of the adhesive is also essential, and for this purpose Plasticine or other forms of modelling clay can be employed. Setting-times vary considerably, from the few seconds of IS12, via the five minutes or so of Devcon type epoxies, to the several hours required by Araldite under normal temperatures, and these times should be taken into consideration when planning your modelling. It is equally as desirable to keep your work clean and uncluttered when using adhesives as it is for soldering operations, but the employment of such bonding agents does permit the incorporation into your models of materials that are unsuit-

able for soldering. Glass fibre resins and other fillers of a non-metallic nature, such as Green Putty or Humbrol Body Putty, can in many cases be used with success in converting metal miniatures, but here again they should not be applied until soldering, if any, is completed. Adhesives having styrene, ketone, acetone or chloroform bases are, generally speaking, unsuitable for metal bonding, and should be used as little as possible in this type of work. Carbon-tetrachloride produces toxic fumes, particularly where heat is involved, and, in my firm opinion, should never be used.

It will be seen that, with a few exceptions, some of which I have mentioned, there is a wide variety of materials suitable for use in metal conversions, and I have found a useful rule of thumb to be 'if it can be bonded and meets requirements, then use it'.

Let us now consider two actual conversion exercises, one fairly simple and one more complex, using Britains' metal models as their bases. Both were produced because of needs in my collection which could not be satisfied by the use of standard pieces. They will give you a good impression of what is involved in these types of conversion, then you can let your imagination loose in the realisation of your own projects.

Conversion 1

This was to produce a British infantry officer in full-dress c1900, standing easy. The basic figure chosen for conversion was Britains' astride officer with moveable arms, holding binoculars, and it was treated for paint removal in the way that has been described earlier in this chapter. Both arms, in fact a one piece casting, were removed with great care and put aside in the spares box for future use, and the head was cut off at the level of the collar top edge. All moulded equipment detail, except the waist-belt, was then taken off with a very fine-toothed file, as was the sword-scabbard attached to the left leg, and the front opening of the tunic was cut in more sharply. Removal of the pistol holster and binocular case left the casting shell rather thin at these points, so it was reinforced with a light application of solder which was immediately filed down to blend in with the surrounding areas. The soldering iron was then used to build up the officer's sash, passing over the left shoulder, around the body, and having two tassels hanging above the right hip, somewhat to the rear. Sash edges were trimmed straight and tassel detail cut in using a sharp scriber, before the same process was used to make the shoulder-cords.

Having drilled out the collar and formed a solder neck-spigot on the head, this latter was trial-fitted to the torso to ascertain the best angle, but was not permanently secured. The overall pose had, of course, been worked out before conversion started, so suitable arms were found in the scrap box. The left one was cut at the elbow, bent, and soldered in its new configuration, and the hands were adjusted at the wrist for correct positioning. Slight readjustment of hand positions can often be achieved merely by twisting gently, two pairs of pliers being employed, their jaws covered with thickish sheet lead or wash-leather to avoid bruising items gripped in them, one to hold the forearm steady, the other to move the hand. More extreme movement will, however, usually require the hand to be severed at the wrist then re-fixed in the desired position.

Both arms were then soldered to the shoulders, and the joints were filed down and smoothed over. Some grooving at shoulders and elbows was carried out to represent folds in the cloth of the tunic. Then the sword and scabbard were constructed from brass wire beaten flat, the hilt guard was made from a small piece of lead sheet, with a sword-knot built up with solder, and both items were fixed in place, the scabbard having slings of thin brass shim. Lastly, the head was fitted and secured, and when this had been done and a final check made of the smoothness and efficacy of all joints, the figure was complete ready for painting. Before the undercoating was applied, the model was treated all over with polyurethane varnish, well brushed in and serving as a protection against the attacks of 'lead disease'. Painting itself was deliberately kept simple, with a minimum of shading and highlighting, but with all detail such as belt, sash, buttons and badges outlined to thrown them into deep relief against their backgrounds.

This typical example of minor conversion illustrates how merely changing positions of arm and head, and substituting other equipment, results in an entirely new figure, without radical alteration to the main portion of the original casting.

Conversion 2

For this figure, rather more involved work has been necessary. It represents a mounted officer of British infantry, in the service-dress worn at the beginning of the First World War, and makes use of parts from several Britains' castings, plus a metal head, pistol-holster, sword, and horse's tail from the Rose Models range. Here is a breakdown of the parts: horse's head from the mounted model of HM The Queen; horse's chest and fore-legs, hindquarters and rear legs from the mounted Huntswoman (Hunt Series); horse's barrel, (mid-portion), plus legs and lower torso of man, from the mounted policeman (Farm Series); upper torso and arms of man, from the Territorial officer, marching; all these pieces being of Britains' manufacture. The Rose Models items already listed, together with some brass wire and sheet lead, complete the tally of component parts, all of which were cleansed of any paint, and brushed up ready for assembly.

This was commenced by soldering together the four main parts making up the horse and lower portion of the rider. The fore and hind quarters were soldered to the barrel, the moulded tail having been removed and the gap closed with solder, then all seams, casting marks, and the moulded trademark were filed smooth, caution being taken not to obliterate the animal's musculature, and to ensure that it stood squarely on all four hooves. The head and neck were then soldered on, the seam treated as before, and the moulded detail of the ceremonial bridle was cut off to leave a standard service bridle. At this stage, the rider's legs were lengthened slightly with solder, and the feet were carved to make more acceptable boots. Stirrups and short leathers were fabricated from wire and soldered into place, with small pieces of wire let into the boot heels to serve as spurs. Next the man's upper torso complete with Sam Browne belt was soldered on, the arms having been bent and secured into their new positions, with a wire riding-whip fitted to the right hand, and the collar drilled out ready for the new head. The pistol holster was fixed to the right side of the belt, and an ammunition pouch was built up from solder on the left side. Solder was also used to form the binocular-case descending from the right rear of the saddle.

Fine brass wire was beaten flat into strip, and fitted to the horse as reins and breast-strap, a wire bit having been inserted in a hole drilled through the head at the top of the mouth fold. More wire, looped and twisted, made the head-rope round the neck and attached to the bridle under the animal's 'chin'. Another hole was drilled in the hindquarters, and the Rose Models tail was inserted and secured, before the sword was attached to the left rear of the saddle. Sheet lead was folded and strapped with flattened wire, then fitted over the holster and rear arch of the saddle to make the rider's coat and valise. Last of all, the head casting was secured, all work was checked, and the completed item was treated with polyurethane varnish in preparation for painting.

Whilst you may not necessarily wish to carry out an exact copy of this conversion, the kinds of components used and the sequence followed in its assembly will help you to work out your own ideas.

A good deal, indeed probably all, of the work I have described as having been done with the soldering iron could have been effected by means of adhesives of one kind or another, provided care was taken in the matching up of parts to be joined, fillers were used to fill any gaps, and all excess adhesive was cleaned off the model before painting.

By following the advice given in this chapter, you will be able to make the best use of your surplus, damaged, or incomplete Britains' metal miniatures.

SECTION THREE

Introduction

Any book which tried to cover every possible facet of making, painting, animating, converting and collecting every type of model figure in every conceivable scale and material would, of necessity, be three times the length and price of this volume! However, in the preceding pages we have shown how to work with and from figures in the two most popular materials, plastic and metal, and a variety of the most popular scales.

There are, of course, a number of 'odd' scale figures produced by individual manufacturers around the world, ranging from the diminutive Heroics 1:300 scale models about ⅛" tall to huge 300mm figures, embracing in passing, 15, 40 and 60mm scales. The scope is practically endless.

The two chapters which follow describe features of figure modelling which are applicable to all types of model, regardless of materials or scale. Then finally there is a chapter on how to cast your own figures in metal; and one on carving them from wood.

There are alternatives to even these, of course. Model figures *can* be made of practically any material which can be cast, moulded, carved, cut and cemented or soldered. As examples, superb models can and have been made using those two materials most of us encounter in primary school—Plasticine and Plaster of Paris.

The potential of Plasticine is frequently underrated since it cannot be successfully hardened and has a tendency to dry out and crack with age. However, if a basic 'stick figure' is made from stiff wire first, and the Plasticine moulded around this to the desired shape, the first problem can be overcome with little difficulty; while sealing the material by brushing the completed figure over with Humbrol Banana Oil prevents cracking. Sealing Plasticine in this way also provides a firm surface on which normal modelling paints will adhere perfectly, though of course painting is not essential with Plasticine since the coloured materials themselves can be mixed to produce any tone or shading required—with practice.

Plaster of Paris is another versatile medium which can easily be cast using the simplest of moulds, and, of course, it does not require any heat to make it set. Moulds for moulding plaster figures can themselves be made from Plaster of Paris using a master figure in the same way as described by Donald Featherstone later for metal figures. The problem with Plaster of Paris is that it will not take deep undercuts, so a fairly simple figure with his arms close to his body is essential.

And too, there is absolutely no reason whatsoever why you should not mix materials in the same figure. If it produced the result you wanted, there would be no harm in a model with, say, metal legs, a wooden body and a plastic head—or any variation thereof! The only way to tackle the problem of a particular model is to study the painting or photograph you are working from; have a look through manufacturers' catalogues and the shelves in your local shops to see whether there are *any* figures or components which can be utilised as some form of basis; and plan construction of the rest depending on your skill in working with various materials, the time available and the tools in your workshop. As has been said elsewhere in this book, figure modelling is a very individual hobby and the limits of what can be achieved lie purely in your own imagination and skills.

eleven

'Mac' Kennaugh
Horse anatomy and animation

Since most modellers are aware of other people around them all the time, and are acquainted with their own physiques in mirrors, they usually have a basic knowledge of human anatomy which is reflected in their figures (although one does see some superb 'double-jointed' howlers). However, for most people horses are four-legged beasts occasionally glimpsed from car or train window, and consequently they have only the vaguest ideas of equine anatomy or what a horse actually does with its legs when it is moving. This results in many model horses being forced into the most unnatural, and frequently impossible, postures which the observer's eye often spots as 'wrong' without being able to pin-point exactly why. In this chapter 'Mac' Kennaugh describes, with the help of Ian Heath's illustrations, how a horse 'works', while the 64 drawings of basic postures during movement will enable you to strike a happy pose in any model.

How many times have you seen a beautifully done conversion of a mounted figure which somehow does not look quite right? If you are not particularly knowledgeable about horses it may merely give an uneasy feeling that something is wrong, but you cannot quite make out what it is. The eye and mind are so used to seeing the natural flow and movement in life that only something unusual is likely to strike you as not right or out of place, and though many a countryman will spot the error at once the 'townie' is likely to be left wondering. This chapter is intended to ensure that if you tackle horse conversions you will not be caught out.

Everything capable of movement has some form of restriction placed on its movement by its own body, and in the case of creatures with bones, these restrictions are set by muscle, and more important, bone movements. We know that acrobats are often unusually supple and in many cases 'double-jointed', and their limbs can be made to bend against the more usual directions of nature. But we would not normally convert a human figure to have the arm bent back at the elbow joint, or the neck rotated 90 degrees, so why do the equivalent with a horse?

The first thing is to get an idea of the basic anatomy of the horse and thus be able to know how the body can move or be moved.

Starting at the head, first the ears. These have no skeletal structure and are moved by muscles which permit them to angle back and forward and pivot. In the 'pricked' position as illustrated the ears form roughly a right-angle to a line from the 'poll' (which is the centre top of the head) to the mouth centre. Their movement range in this plane to the 'laid back' position is about 90 degrees. When moving from the pricked to laid back position the ear also rotates outwards through rather less than 90 degrees. The ears move

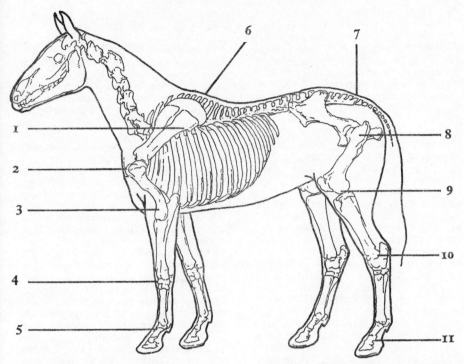

*Basic horse anatomy—numbers
are referred to in text.*

independently in these directions so any combination is possible in theory, though a combination of the extremes is less likely.

With ears pricked the horse is alert or calm, looking with interest at something, and generally well collected. With both flat, the horse is under some form of stress, anger, fear or violent action, and it is often significant of a situation the horse does not like.

Next the head itself. This is pivoted at the end of the neck and can twist sideways about 25 degrees each way and up and down through about 95 degrees. When the head stretches forward the muzzle is lifted and vice versa. The position of the head in relation to the body is used as a balance weight by the horse, and unless the horse can stretch his head right forward he cannot run at full speed or 'full stretch', hence reining-in slows a horse down. I will mention here that I am simplifying a great deal to make it easy for the layman—perhaps those reading who are riding enthusiasts will forgive this.

Now the neck. Many will be surprised from the drawing at just where the neck bones are, particularly where they join the spine. The neck, of course, can flex in a twisting motion and bend up and down. When bending, each segment of the neck moves so the whole moves in a curved manner though the movement of the head into the up position will straighten the neckbones. The important item is the pivot point on the spine. Most people think the neck pivots above the shoulders where the pommel of the saddle fits. Not so, the pivot point is in fact nearer the chest, and this is why so many conversions to make a horse with a lowered head drooped to the ground look odd. The modeller has made his pivot at the withers and then found the head won't reach the ground so makes the neck longer—hence giraffe-necked horses. If, in fact, the neck is lowered to a position where the lower end of the windpipe is about ¾ way down the chest the conversion will look right. With head lowered the collar of bone which is the horse's shoulder can be clearly seen as the lower part of the neck is thick flesh, and the chest and underside of the neck (throat) muscle and flesh with the windpipe prominent from the head to chest.

Now taking the foreleg, the upper joint (1) is the shoulder. This joint has a limited movement back and forward and can move slightly sideways to 'splay' the forelegs. Next the main upper joint (2) which is the upper elbow. This has a normal movement through about 90 degrees though it can move more when forced.

Joint 3, the elbow, has virtually no forward movement as it locks like our knee joint when forward, but can bend right up to close the joint—about 100 degrees.

Now the knee (4), which again has no forward movement as it locks straight but will bend back through about 100 degrees to close the joint like our own knee. Finally the bone formation forming the ankle and foot (5). These bones are complex and normally pivot back about 80 degrees, but there is a cartilage shock absorber which will allow more movement forward to absorb shocks.

Turning to the spine from 6 to 7, this can move slightly from side to side on a well suppled horse and can hump up in a surprisingly tight curve when the horse really bucks. The region of greatest lateral flexion is in front of the rear quarters.

Hind legs. Here there are no shoulder blades as with the forelegs, but a hip joint which can move forward and aft through about 120 degrees—rather more forward than aft (8). Lower we have the thigh joint, which is in fact the horse's knee and has a knee cap, so thigh is not correct even if the joint is something of a knee/thigh cross. This joint moves mainly in conjunction with the hip and has more movement aft (9). Now the hock which never straightens but moves only forward (10), and finally the rear foot which moves as the forefeet (11). The rear leg is rather less flexible in motion than the fore, and normal movements tend to produce a set combination of joint positions. The whole body is, of course, surprisingly flexible, as anyone who has seen a horse roll in a field or bite his rump knows, and the shock absorbing qualities of the limbs enable the horse, saddle and rider to be sprung vertically in the air and landed stiff-legged with a jolt sufficient to remove a limpet.

Having now (I hope) given some idea of what moves how, we will move on to consider the horse in motion and see just how the limbs operate in those combinations providing the differing gaits.

The horse in motion

For many years until the invention of photography, indeed until the development of slow motion photography, there was controversy over the positions of a horse's legs in motion, and indeed many artists had portrayed horses with both fore- and hind-legs wide splayed to depict the gallop. Now we know exactly how the movements take place but it is surprising how many modellers make mistakes in altering horses, and even the manufacturers' sculptors are not always perfect.

It is very important to remember that at any point in time an object, be it fixed or movable, is in a normal state of balance. A fixed object must be balanced or it will fall, and similarly a moving object must be balanced both statically and dynamically (in other words, its centre of gravity must not reach a position where movement is unable to retain that position, or the movement must not become such that the centre of gravity is forced into an unbalanced position). To illustrate what is meant: a runner trips over something and unless he is able to accelerate his forward movement to 'catch up'—or restore his centre of gravity to a position of balance—he falls. If he can accelerate he retains a state of balance where it is restored by different movement—in this case faster movement.

The horse has four normal paces, walk, trot, canter and gallop. It is essential to show these paces by illustration or the explanation becomes too complicated.

The Walk

This is a 'four beat' pace. A 'beat' is the point at which a foot is placed firmly on the ground and consequently in a position for impulsion. In some paces the impulsion is mainly from the hind legs and this should be so in the walk. Each leg is lifted and placed down separately, but in a definite sequence. Properly trained, a ridden horse should commence to walk with a hind leg so, if started with the near hind (the *left* side is the near side), the sequence is 1—near hind, 2—near fore, 3—off hind and 4—off fore. Referring to the illustrations, as the near hind is placed on the ground (1 and 2), the near fore moves forward to take the weight in position 4 (the

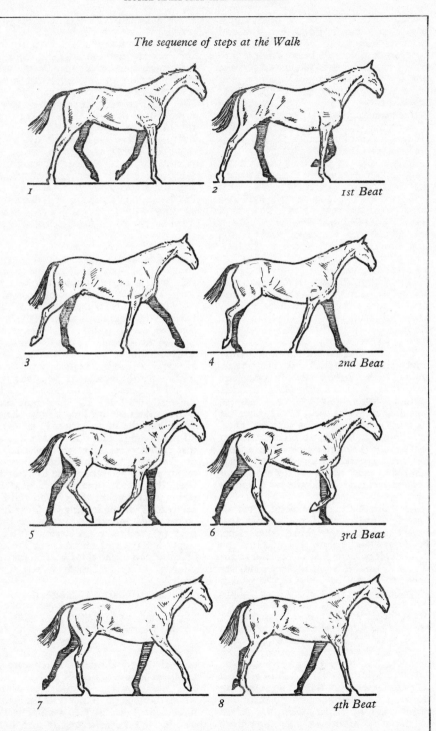

The sequence of steps at the Walk

1

2

1st Beat

3

4

2nd Beat

5

6

3rd Beat

7

8

4th Beat

second beat) while the off hind moves back to position in 3 and then in 4 and 5 moves forward to take the weight in position 6, the third beat. The off fore which is following sequence behind the positions of the off hind then moves forward in 5, 6 and 7 to take the weight in 8, the fourth beat. The cycle then commences again with the repeat of beat 1. The explanation sounds complicated but reading in conjunction with the illustrations clarifies the matter.

It is important to remember that the intermediate positions to those illustrated are subject to alteration on *all* leg positions. For instance, if you wanted a horse with the near foreleg in a more forward position than illustration 2, then the legs would all move towards the positions in 3 (ie off fore more to rear, near hind more to rear and off hind just clear of the ground).

Notice that at the walk the head will normally be carried in a relaxed pose and note also that the rider will be upright and relaxed.

The Trot

This pace is often one which is slightly unnatural for a horse and many badly trained horses have a slovenly trot. The pace is a beat of two time with the horse springing alternately from one pair of legs diagonally opposed, to the other. At its most exaggerated it is seen on 'pace' or 'Trotting' horses, sometimes known as 'Yankee Trotters', where the animal has been specially trained to an exaggerated trot gait where the leg movement is greatly extended and the horse moves very rapidly indeed.

At the trot there is a point when all four feet are clear of the ground just before each alternate 'beat' takes place. Positions 1 and 5 show this, and in 1 the pair of legs referred to as the right diagonal, the off fore and near hind, are about to be placed down. As this takes place (2) the legs of the left diagonal are moving forward (2, 3 and 4), and as they reach the forward stretched position the horse impels clear of the ground with a spring landing on the left diagonal and continuing the cycle. The bouncy motion of the trot is, of course, imparted to the rider, who has the choice of sitting, when he remains seated in the saddle absorbing the 'shock' of the motion by the flexibility of his body, or 'rising', when he lifts up to the trot, absorbing the motion by

moving himself. This is referred to as posting. When posting the rider leans his body slightly forward as he is going with the motion, and additionally he must remain in dynamic balance so the more rapid forward movement brings a forward shift in his own centre of gravity. The illustrations well show that certain positions in the trot are not ideal from the modelling point of view, as they are not graceful and the appearance of movement is momentarily lost. Pick the positions where the horse looks in motion. Note also that the bounding movement will impart itself to mane and tail and any loose accoutrements on saddlery etc, so to give the true effect of motion this must be shown on the model.

The Canter

This is a most natural and graceful pace. Most horses moving freely in a field will canter from point to point, but when ridden the canter is often hard to hold until a rider is experienced. This is because the rider tends to impel the horse forward into a gallop. The canter is a beat of three time. The horse leads off with either near fore or off fore leg. With a near fore lead the sequence will be off hind, right diagonal, near fore; and with an off fore lead, will be near hind, left diagonal, off fore. The first beat illustrated shows the off hind firmly planted propelling the horse forward and taking all the weight. The other three legs are just commencing to move forward. The off fore and near hind (right diagonal) will come to the ground next in 3 (second beat), by which time the off hind has commenced to clear the ground and lifts the rear (4) as the leading leg (near fore) is stretched forward to make the third beat (5) and take the weight (6) and impulsion (7) and on reaching the end of impulsion of the third beat all four are clear of the ground ready to restart the cycle.

It is essential that when modelling horses at the canter the sequence is understood and that if a position is chosen where the fore foot or hind foot is shown firmly on the ground the precise position of the other legs depends on which leg is down. In other words, if the horse is leading near or off fore. There is a gait known as a 'disunited canter' when the legs go astray and the gait is unbalanced, but that is a complication we shall ignore as a well trained horse

Two views of Roy Dilley's magnificent diorama depicting a group of soldiers from the Duke of Cornwall's Light Infantry during a break in training on Bodmin Moor in the 1880s. Note the very realistic effects which can be achieved using small chippings of loose shale and lichen. The 'flowers' were made from paintbrush bristles while the 'grass' is model railway accessory grass matting.

Above *Roy Dilley's diorama of a jeep and trailer with crew in Normandy, 1944, constructed as described in Chapter 10.* **Below** *Stages in the home-moulding process as detailed by Donald Featherstone. The top photo shows a mould box of Lego with the front removed; a plastic card box with the front cut-away to show the pattern embedded in the Plasticine; and at rear a cut plastic card box shown before folding around a Plasticine block. The bottom picture shows two Silastomer mounds with the figures cast from them. In the background, two halves of mould are shown clamped in a sandwich between hardboard pieces.*

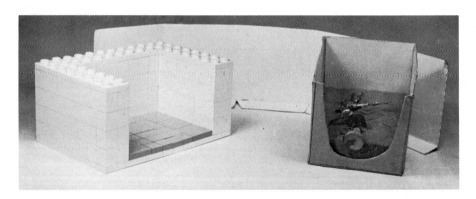

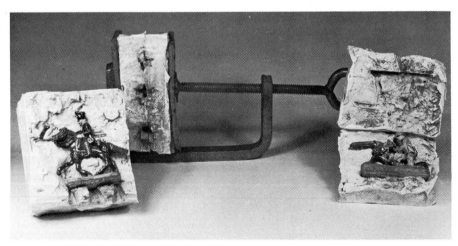

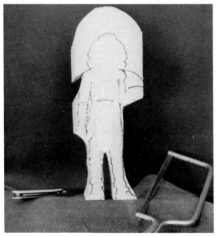

First stages in carving the Aztec warrior.
Top left *Front and side views of figure drawn onto paper divided into one inch squares.* **Top right** *Outline of figure's front traced onto wood.* **Above** *Beginning to cut out the figure.* **Above right** *Cardboard template of figure side view used to provide side outline on wood block.* **Right** *Shape and round the figure using dividers to check proportions with the drawing.*

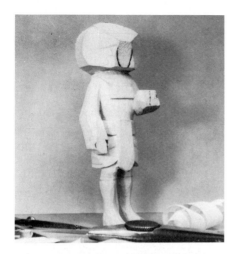

Left *Cut left arm to protrude from the body and cut away surplus wood from the legs.* **Below left** *Drill holes through both hands to hold weapon and shield, and carve in finer details.* **Below** *Aztec figure ready for painting.*

The sequence of steps at the Trot

1

2   *1st Beat—right diagonal*

3

4

5

6   *2nd Beat—left diagonal*

7

8

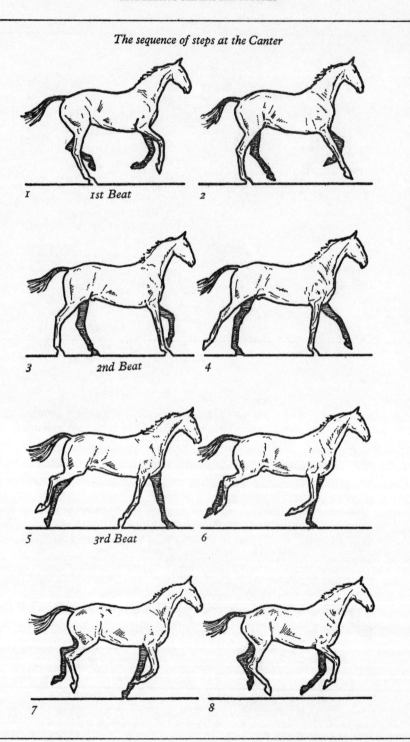

The sequence of steps at the Canter

1   1st Beat   2

3   2nd Beat   4

5   3rd Beat   6

7   8

The sequence of steps at the Gallop

1   *1st Beat*   2

3   *2nd Beat*   4   *3rd Beat*

5   6   *4th Beat*

7   8

and rider should never get so mixed up! At the canter the rider will again be upright as moving his weight forward will throw the horse into a gallop.

The Gallop

From the modelling angle, this is probably the most important, as the charging cavalryman is the popular action figure. When a horse at a canter increases his speed and stretches forward he reaches a point where the diagonals cannot be put down together so he 'breaks' the three beat pace into a four beat pace and the sequence becomes near hind, off hind, near fore, off fore. The illustrations show that in the second beat (3) the off hind is down while the near fore, well stretched, is not yet in position but follows to make the third beat (4), and the off fore makes the fourth beat (6) which after completion (7) is followed by a period of suspension (8) with all feet off the ground. The illustrations show a horse leading with the off fore and of course the leg positions alter as described previously when he leads near fore. The rider leans forward at the gallop and the horse stretches forward with the motion. A horse at a controlled gallop looks very much more sedate than one taking part in a wild gallop, and often a cavalry horse would be little more than an uncontrolled and terrified animal generally aimed in one direction by a rider concerned with his own chances. The head and neck would be stretched far forward, ears flat back and eyes rolling with lots of white showing, mane and tail flying. Careful choice of the pose can help impart a feel of action about a figure and just three or four figures well posed can give a feeling of a hectic charge better than many more ill-positioned.

It is hoped that this gives the less informed a better idea of just what a moving horse should look like, and for those who want to undertake conversions of stock horses into fresh positions but have not yet developed the 'feel' for movement needed for a successful result, the use of this article and some 'matchstick' sketches of the proposed positions will soon show if you are right or wrong *before* you start cutting.

twelve

Roy Dilley
Dioramas and scenic work

The incorporation of model figures in groups on scenic bases is growing in popularity as the number of figures available for all historical periods increases. Instead of a model soldier being displayed in isolation on a plinth or in a glass cabinet, he may be placed with a number of his fellows, all in different positions, to give the effect of some natural activity being carried out. These groups, or 'dioramas', can vary from a simple composition involving two or three men drinking in a bar, say, to large and complicated scenes involving masses of figures in the representation of some dramatic military situation. The correct composition of a diorama is one of the most difficult techniques to learn, the most common pitfall being crowding together so many figures and accessories that the overall effect is one of sheer confusion. In this chapter, Roy Dilley explains his own approach and techniques, and although he concentrates on 54mm, his ideas are equally applicable to any scale.

Military miniatures are, like all other 'objets d'art', intended for display or exhibition for the interest, information, and gratification of the viewer. It follows that, the more striking the display, the more effective is the impression that it makes upon the observer. In the earlier days of collecting, enthusiasts generally relied for their display effect upon large numbers of models, massed in formation as if paraded for a review, and the results were often surprisingly successful. Backgrounds, with some exceptions, tended to be quite simple, with little attempt to represent accurately details of ground or architecture, the main requirement being a base, as nearly flat as possible, upon which the ranks of what were virtually still only 'toy' figures could be marshalled with some stability. Even slight irregularities in the surface of the base could precipitate disastrous situations if it were knocked or vibrated, since a tilted figure could lose its equilibrium very easily and topple against its neighbour causing it to fall in its turn against another, and so on right across the layout in an overwhelming 'snowball' reaction.

Nowadays, however, with the tremendous increases in the standards of modelling and attention to detail that have developed in recent years, a great deal more emphasis is being laid upon the backgrounds against which models are displayed and the scenic settings into which they are incorporated. The accent at the present time is on realism in models of all kinds, and requires realistic treatment of their environmental circumstances. Even an item individually mounted on a minimum of base or stand area becomes more convincing if the 'ground' surface upon which it is standing has been properly and appropriately textured.

Massed displays of a parade nature are, of course, still with us, and very satisfactory they can be, but there is an increasing tendency among military modellers to depict groups of personnel and/or equipment of various kinds in miniature settings, as accurately as possible reproducing the appearance of real life. Where actual incidents are being portrayed a great deal of trouble is taken to ensure that the models appear in the correct circumstances of location and terrain, and some outstandingly plausible presentations have been achieved. It is obvious that, just as in real life men and animals together with all their weaponry and other impedimenta exist in, and are affected to a greater or lesser extent by their surroundings, so models of personnel and equipment will gain validity from accurate representation of these environmental factors.

As modellers have turned more and more to the use of scenic settings, or dioramas, as they are universally known, manufacturers of aids and accessories have shown some diligence in the provision of materials to make the construction of scenery easier and more true to life. Thus it is now possible to obtain pre-formed bases representing many kinds of ground surface, model trees and buildings in various scales, printed and embossed papers and card in the likenesses of different types of stone and brickwork, other papers with scale grasslike appearance, and accessories in great variety, from oil-drums and jerricans to tow-chains and furniture. Techniques have also been evolved in which use is made of as many 'natural' textures and structures as can be pressed into service, so that mosses, tiny plants, rock fragments, twigs and so on play their parts in the miniaturisation of scenic features.

These 'natural' materials are, if carefully and appropriately employed, usually more effective than manufactured items, and, although some may not always be readily available, especially to the town dwelling modeller, holidays and out of town visits and trips will often provide opportunities for amassing a supply of useful items. Experienced modellers get into the habit of keeping a sharp lookout for plants, rocks, twigs, and other materials that can be utilised for scenic work, and some go to the extent of actually cultivating in their gardens small plants that provide a permanent source of particular textures and structures. Some scenic features can be reproduced satisfactorily by artificial means however, and, as in the creation of other models, it is the skilful blending of the most effective materials, natural or artificial, in a scene which determines its success.

Whilst always striving for maximum realism in settings, the modeller should guard against letting his enthusiasm run away with him to the extent of allowing them to dominate the models that they are intended to set off and complement. The aim should therefore be to establish a situation of rapport between subject and setting, in accordance with the artistic principles of composition.

How then is one to set about the construction of a diorama or scenic group? Basically, such a work will be one of two types, either 'open' and viewable from all sides and above, or 'closed' and to be viewed only from one side, to all intents and purposes a three-dimensional framed 'picture'. In the former case, groundwork and scenic features will be in the correct dimensional relationship to the model in terms of scale and distance, whilst in the latter instance, questions of perspective, angle and background may apply, as well as those of lighting. Beginners in the art may feel that the open type of scene is the one with which they can best gain experience, and certainly this is the style in which the majority of scenic groups are executed. 'Open' or 'closed', however, the scene needs a subject, and a grouping of models and surroundings that will make an effective, realistic presentation, preferably establishing a situation, or, as it were, telling some kind of 'story'.

Actual incidents from history, especially when they have been well-documented or illustrated, present admirable opportunities for 'getting things right'. Prints, photographs, maps, and descriptive accounts are of great assistance in providing accurate data on attitudes, uniforms, equipment and locations, it merely being necessary to establish the extent of the groundwork in which the models are to be placed. Some exceptional work has been done in this respect, by interpreting in the round famous paintings or photographs, and such scenes, provided the original source is accurate and reliable, give great satisfaction to their creators and viewers alike.

More often, a modeller makes use of

his own imagination and knowledge of a period or particular action to construct a scenic group without an actual illustration from which to work. In such a case, stances, positions of equpment, and, to some extent, the ground itself are the products of what the modeller knows might have been happening, or was typical of the general situation at a certain time, and allow freedom of expression in the production of an interpretation that is uniquely personal. The more an enthusiast can develop an awareness of the 'feel' of a specific era or moment in history, the more likely it is that he will be able to convey that feeling to others via his work.

Remember too that military life is not all ceremonial parades and violent action. A great many of the best dioramas evocative of a soldier's existence have concerned themselves with its domestic, routine, recreational, and even humorous aspects, all of which offer ideal material. It is, in my opinion, as important to take the utmost care in the conception and planning of a scenic group, as it is in the execution of the piece, and time spent in this way is seldom wasted. Knowing what you are trying to achieve, and having a good picture in your mind's eye of the layout and detail that is to be incorporated into your diorama, saves much disappointment, false starting, and misspent effort.

Some top-class exponents of the art, when planning a project, try to think themselves right into the scene, picturing themselves in the position of one of the key figures in the composition, and allowing the details of attitude, activity and placement to form around that concept. It really all comes down to imagination and the capacity to 'freeze' a situation at that certain point that is to be depicted. After that, it becomes a matter of applying skills and techniques in the translation of the mind picture into the physical reality. Start with simple subjects and progress to more complex work when you have a better knowledge of your abilities. Learn from other people's experience, and do not hestitate to ask questions of expert modellers, most of whom are only too pleased to share their know-how and methods.

Having decided upon the subject and extent of the diorama, and whether it is to be of the open or closed variety, it is useful to make some rough sketches of the layout, and from them to calculate overall dimensions etc, and the positioning of groundwork and models, bearing in mind at this stage the space available for the eventual display of the piece. How disconcerting it can be to launch oneself into the construction of an ambitious project only to realise that there is nowhere that it can conveniently be housed when completed! It also makes sense to consider scenic features in conjunction with the models, since the stances of men and animals, and the placement of vehicles and guns, will be affected in some degree by the nature of the ground which they occupy, and any necessary adjustments can be made. Several courses then lie open to the modeller. He can proceed to complete the setting before making his models and fitting them into place; he can finish the models and use them in the construction of his scenic effects; or, and this to my mind is the preferable way, he can develop both together, so that the final positions of models and features of the setting can be firmly established before painting and finishing are carried out, and all component parts are united in the completed work. The modeller's personal preference, however, will determine which course he follows, since what suits one person may well not be acceptable to another, and the overriding aim of modelling is, after all, to enjoy what one is doing!

An essential for a successful diorama is a good firm base upon which groundwork can be built up and models mounted, with complete confidence that it will stand up to the weight and to subsequent conditions of handling and possible transportation. For this purpose a stout base-board, plywood, chipboard or similar, sufficiently thick to resist warping is ideal. Anything of a flimsy or flexible nature, polystyrene ceiling tiles, cardboard and the like, should be avoided as base materials, although they may well be useful in the construction of detail on the more substantial boards that I have recommended.

Ideally, one side of the base should be covered with a sheet of baize, felt, or flock-paper to provide an undersurface that will not scratch any polished areas of tables, cabinets and the like upon which the diorama may later be displayed. The other side should be scored to make a key for the groundwork that is to be applied. This latter can be made up basically from layers of expanded polystyrene glued together with PVA adhesive, Unibond, Elmer's, Durofix or similar, and carved to shape: from blocks of balsa or other wood similarly treated; or from plaster, self-hardening putties of the DAS type, or builder's spackle, coated over wood or compressed paper formers. If the last method is employed, the wooden surface of the base board must, after scoring, be treated with a sealant against the penetration of water from the plaster, which will otherwise cause warping to occur.

Ditches, trenches, roads, shell holes and other depressions can be cut into the groundwork, and rises, mounds and banks built up. When this contouring has been accomplished, with any relevant checking against the models that are to be incorporated, the texturing and surfacing can be applied, and details of scenery, walls, hedges, trees, buildings and the rest can be fabricated. This is where skill in the use of natural and manufactured scenic accessories comes into its own, and where ingenuity and improvisation can be exercised.

Sphagnum mosses, bunched together and glued into grooves cut into the ground surface, make splendid hedges, or, attached to twigs, serve well as foliage. The root systems of certain tree seedlings bear a striking similarity to the patterns made by the boughs and branches of full sized trees, and such seedlings, dried and treated with a transparent sealer or varnish, make ideal models of deciduous trees in their winter state. Moss, dyed sawdust, or scraps of sponge foam glued to the root tendrils represents foliage very well, as do lichens, and even dried used tea leaves, suitably dyed or coloured. There are many proprietary kits of evergreen trees such as pines and firs, and coconut and date palms can be obtained in the Britains tree ranges.

Long grass can be simulated with lengths of unravelled hempen string, or brush bristles of varying thicknesses, and the same materials, dipped at one end in glue then sprinkled with sand or sawdust, can be made to serve as corn or reeds. Flock scattered over white PVA glue, or proprietary scenic matting papers, will solve the problem of representing ordinary short grass, whilst mown lawns can again be portrayed by fine velvety flock-papers. As I have stated earlier in this chapter, miniature plants can be dried and used to great effect as scenic items, as can rocks, stones, and pieces of wood and twigs.

Earth is best counterfeited with coarse sand, sprinkled over a coating of white glue, and painted in the appropriate shade when dry. Sandy surfaces pose no problems, since sand is able to serve as itself without difficulty. Although awkward to represent with fidelity, snow can be made quite satisfactorily with a mixture of salt, alum, and plaster.

Walls, buildings, cobbled roads and many other architectural features can be obtained as kits, or ready formed accessories, or they can be fabricated with wood or plastic, plaster coated or covered with printed building papers or textured card.

Perhaps the most difficult of all scenic types to model, thick jungle, has been attempted successfully by utilising dried ferns of the maidenhair and other miniature varieties, and dyeing them before incorporation into the scene. All in all, there is no limit to the opportunities for the exercise of skill and ingenuity in the realistic representation of scenery.

Here, as exercises, are examples of dioramas which may help you to develop your techniques in this aspect of modelling. The first provides a background for a model of a jeep and trailer with its crew, and shows a stretch of country track in Normandy after the Invasion of 1944.

The base board in this case was purchased ready-made from the Soldier Centre at Oxford, England, and came complete with baize undersurface and veneered edges. However, it could have been prepared as I have described earlier. The top was scored and brushed over with sealer, which was allowed to dry thoroughly. Next, a quantity of Das self-hardening modelling clay was pressed over the surface, and well into the scored keying indentations, the overall thickness being about a quarter of an inch, but varying slightly from place to place to represent the undulations of the track. A little clean water was brushed over the Das, and a pair of spare jeep wheels, fitted at the correct track distance on a wooden axle, were run to and fro across the surface, leaving realistic tyre-marked ruts. Similarly,

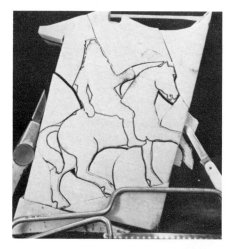

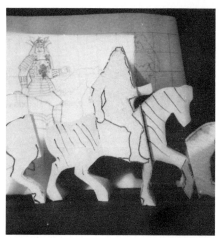

First stages in carving the Samurai. **Top left** *Front and side views drawn on paper.* **Top right** *Side view of figure traced on to block of wood, showing also preliminary cuts.* **Above** *Side view cut out.* **Above right** *Cut away a thin slice of wood from each side of the horse as shaded to leave the figure's legs standing out.* **Right** *Cut away surplus wood to divide the horse's legs.*

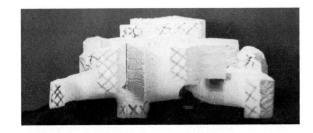

View of underside of man and horse showing where sections have been cut away.

Shape horse's head and tail and round off body.

Begin to shape and round off the Samurai figure's body.

Above *Drill holes through hands for bow and horse's reins and trim in further detail, using a pair of dividers to check the proportions against the drawings.* **Right** *Begin the painting process as shown with the torso before finishing off the helmet or adding the bow and other detail items.*

Painting is well under way in these two views of Martin Rendall's 'War Lord', which drew admiring crowds to the British Model Soldier Society stand at the Model Engineer Exhibition in 1975. Note that helmet details have now been added together with a sword though the bow and reins are not attached until last.

footmarks were impressed into the material on either side of the track, a pair of Historex legs providing the means to accomplish this, the boots having well defined soles and heels.

The jeep model had initially been placed on the track to check its final position in relation to the ruts and edges, and had been removed whilst the treatment of the base proceeded. An old shaving brush provided nicely tapered bristles, which were pushed in bunches well into the Das along one edge of the track, outside the footmarks, and made very convincing clumps of coarse grass. The clay was then left to set absolutely dry and hard, and was afterwards painted completely over with Humbrol Dark Earth matt enamel. All the clumps of 'grass' were coloured a faded green with pale yellowed tips, appropriate to the summer period being depicted, and for this Campaign oil-bound poster colours were used. Dark earth paint was also applied as mud to the jeep wheels before the vehicle was cemented into its pre-determined position on the base, all other painting and weathering having been completed previous to this operation. Finally, clear varnish was brushed into ruts, tyre treads and marks, and footmarks, and, very sparingly, here and there on the surface of the track to give an 'after rain' appearance. This is a very basic piece of scenic work, yet it sets off the vehicle and its crew extremely well.

The second diorama depicts a group of soldiers of the Duke of Cornwall's Light Infantry, during a break in training on Bodmin Moor in the 1880's. The figures, before painting, were used from time to time in the construction of the background, to help establish positions of detail.

Work commenced with a rectangle of ¾ inch blockboard, measuring 9½ inch by 11 inch, which was scored on the top surface and had baize fitted to the underside. Two strips of ½ inch square balsa wood were glued along one edge of the top surface, with a ¼ inch gap between them, and were then sanded to a rounded shape. This was to form the basis for a bank. Next, the entire top was thinly spread with Green Putty, and a track, approximately 2 inches wide was marked into the putty across the centre of the base, slightly diagonally. After the putty had dried, the track was coated with white glue and

sprinkled with coarse sand pressed well in. More white glue was used liberally in the gap along the top of the bank, and quantities of sphagnum moss were 'planted' into it to simulate a hedge. The variety used reproduces very well the windblown appearance of hedges in that upland district.

All the surface of the ground and bank, excluding the track, was treated with the glue, and then covered with grass matting, manufactured as a model railway accessory by the German firm of Vaupe, and generally available in model shops. This matting was pressed close up to the base of the hedge, having the effect of sealing it firmly in place and covering the edges of the planting gap. Along the junctions of the grass areas with the track were glued small chippings of shale, which represent the stones which are commonly used to mark pathways in districts subject to mists, and where it is inadvisable to wander off a firm surface. Other larger pieces of rock were glued down here and there to serve as boulders, and more moss was attached around them to simulate gorse and bracken.

A finishing touch to the groundwork was provided by clumps of lilies, made up from brush bristles treated with glue and sand and planted along the track side. Finally, strips of veneer were fixed along the edges of the baseboard, sanded smooth, and given a coat of gloss varnish. When the figures had been painted and fitted into place, the scene was complete, and extremely true to life.

Groundwork in a boxed scene follows much the same principles, but includes a 'backdrop', the junction of which with the base should be concealed, a hedge or wall providing a satisfactory means of accomplishing this. Also, the junction of backdrop and sidewalls should be camouflaged, or if this is not appropriate to the scene, rounded to avoid a sharp angled change of direction. If the scene is a deep one front to back, it may be necessary to make some provision for perspective, in which parallel lines appear to converge towards a 'vanishing point' on the horizon. There is insufficient space in this chapter to go into the question of perspective, but the public library is bound to have books dealing with the subject in its Art section. Boxed dioramas may also need lighting arrangements, and possibly some means of ventilation to disperse the heated air.

thirteen

Donald F. Featherstone
Casting your own models

Casting one's own figures in metal is not as daunting a task as many people think, and certainly the satisfaction of making your own—however crude the first attempts—justifies the effort. Donald Featherstone's experience in this field is practically unrivalled since he was making his own wargames armies long before the advent of today's quality commercial figures, and here he gives us all the benefits of his knowledge. Modern mould-making materials considerably simplify the problems which had to be overcome a few years ago, and even the complete novice can learn to turn out figures to be proud of after a little practice. It is worth reiterating Don's very sound warning here though: if you use a commercial figure as a 'master' for your own mould it is illegal to sell your figures; and may well end up by killing the geese which lay the golden eggs.

To make one's own model soldiers is a most attractive proposition, particularly in the large numbers required for wargaming. Metal wargames figures are relatively inexpensive so that they have to be produced in large quantities to justify the expense of buying mould-making material and the relatively fiddling business of making the mould, to say nothing of the onerous casting and figure cleaning-up processes. However, while it is well within the ability of the average military collector to make moulds and turn out his own models, it must be understood that these 'gravity' moulds rarely turn out models of the quality produced by a commercial centrifugal mould.

It is permissible to use commercially produced figures as 'patterns' (or 'masters') providing the resulting models are for private use only because to offer such figures for sale is to lay oneself open to prosecution for infringement of copyright. Some wargames clubs make their own 'club' models using as patterns ranges of commercial figures which they produce in large numbers. This is killing the goose that lays the golden eggs because such abuse of the manufacturer's technical knowledge leaves him little encouragement to become financially involved in other than the most basic best-selling ranges.

A rudimentary method of mould making consists of two pieces of cuttlefish (picked up on the beach or purchased from a pet shop) with the model soldier, which must be a simple one with few undercuts, sandwiched between them. The cuttlefish pieces are pressed together so that an impression is taken of the figure. Then, a run-in is cut, the two pieces of cuttlefish clamped together between similar sized pieces of hardboard, and the molten metal poured in to produce a figure that bears a crude but recognisable resemblance to the original pattern.

Plaster of Paris is a cheap and readily available material for moulds, made by using the same methods as when manufacturing rubber moulds except that a thick creamy mixture of Plaster of Paris is poured into the mould-box instead of the silicone rubber. To keep the two halves of the mould separate from each other, a release-agent of either a soap solution or liquid Vaseline is lightly brushed over the faces of the mould and the retaining walls of the mould-box.

A mould made of Plaster of Paris is a fairly vulnerable affair so that removing the hot casting frequently breaks the mould and destroys the clean cast. The mould can be made stronger by using plaster 'doctored' by two teaspoonfuls of sugar in half a cup of water to each threequarters full cup of plaster. When the plaster mould is dry its faces should be given a coat of Wallseal and allowed to dry, so the plaster is strengthened against breaking in casting, and filling up any minute holes.

When casting, if the first figures are accompanied by a smell of burnt sugar, the mould requires at least another day to dry out. Before casting, smoke the surfaces of the mould and the impression therein with a thick coating of carbon (candle smoke) and then re-apply a fresh coating for every two figures cast.

When molten metal is poured into a damp mould it is forcibly expelled through the pouring-hole, causing considerable damage to ceilings and heads bending over the mould! Make certain the plaster is dry and hard before casting.

Moulds can similarly be made from Polyfilla but will not last as long—from five to 15 figures is usually about the average output before the mould begins to break up. Polyfilla moulds should be dried out in an airing cupboard for at least three days before use.

The availability of Room Temperature Vulcanising (RTV) Silicone Rubber has revolutionised mould making by the amateur. Pouring like thick paint, when a catalytic agent is added this substance hardens into a strong but flexible rubber capable of withstanding temperatures of over 500°F, enabling castings with undercuts to be reproduced and easily released. The best known brands are ICI's Silicoset 100; the Silastic Silicone rubbers made by Dow Corning, and RTV 41 made by General Electric of America. In Great Britain they are sold by Alec Tiranti Ltd, 72 Charlotte Street, London W1P 2AJ, and The Strand Glass Company, Brentway Trading Estate, Brentford, Middlesex. Although more expensive than other Silastics made by Dow Corning, their Silastic G will prove a good investment for models that have deep undercuts and for moulds which will receive a lot of handling while in use. This grade is ideal for flexible moulds as it possesses a medium viscosity; a wide serviceable temperature range and extremely high tear-strength giving tough, long-life moulds.

The catalyst supplied with Silastic G is pink and is the only one that should be used with this grade; the mixing level for Silastic G is constant, being invariably one part by weight of catalyst to ten parts by weight of rubber. With the curing agent added, 1lb of Silastic G RTV Rubber will produce 25 cubic inches of rubber, becoming a pourable fluid capable of filling the most minute crevices and reproducing intricate detail. When catalysed, Silastic G has a more or less fixed curing pattern that allows a working time (the time between catalysation and that point at which the material will no longer flow) of two hours and a curing time (the time elapsing before the mould can be handled) of 24 hours (vulcanising at room temperature 77°F, 25°C) although optimum properties for the mould are not fully developed for 72 hours.

Because Silastic RTV silicone rubber reproduces even the slightest imperfections, the selection of the figure to be produced is most important; the pattern (master-model) must be clean and free of oil or grease with no dirt or particles of foreign matter in corners and crevices. A finer reproduction is obtained from unpainted than painted figures. The pattern will probably be of lead or plastic and it is consoling to know that Silastic RTV will not damage the figure, peeling off without leaving any traces. Some materials cause inhibition of the cure by setting up a surface chemical reaction which stops the curing of the rubber at the points where it touches the pattern. Inhibition is easily recognised because the surface interface becomes gummy or pasty; detail is obliterated and the model needs cleaning with a solvent. Some plastics and modelling clays can cause inhibition but generally, wood, metal, plastic, plaster and stone are compatible with RTV Silicone rubber and can be used without any trouble.

When deep moulds are being made or the pattern contains very deep crevices or extremely fine detail, it is helpful to lower the viscosity of Silastic G by adding thinning fluid. When up to ten per cent (by weight) of Silastic RTV thinner is mixed with the uncatalysed rubber an effect of up to 75 per cent reduction in viscosity can take place without seriously affecting the physical properties of the rubber after curing.

To make a mould, embed the pattern for half its thickness in a block of Plasticine about ¾ inch thick, large enough to take the pattern lying flat, with at least ½ inch clearance at all points. Using the point of a penknife, build the Plasticine around the edges of the figure so that it is embedded for half its thickness. This is perhaps the most important step and experience will bring better results with difficult figures, particularly horses. Try to visualise the *parting line* of the figure when placing the pattern in the Plasticine —this is the line around the pattern at which the mould 'breaks' so that the casting can be withdrawn from its cavity without damaging the mould.

The Plasticine surface need not be flat, but should be built up so as to give the best possible parting line. For example, when moulding horses with standing legs, build up the Plasticine so that all four of the horse's legs are half-embedded and half exposed whilst keeping the rest of the horse, such as the tail, also half exposed. An upraised arm can be supported on a tapered 'shelf' of Plasticine, into which it is half-embedded.

Containing the pattern, the Plasticine surface will be reproduced as the face of one of the two halves of the mould and, if the figure is incorrectly positioned, there will be an undercut so that when casting from the finished mould, it will only be possible to remove the figure by damaging the mould. Incorrect positioning of the pattern will also cause the parting-line or the mould's interfaces not to match so that 'flash' (excess metal) forms around the casting.

Next, cut a strip of tin, waxed-card or brass-shim two inches wide and in length the total of each of the four sides of the Plasticine block *plus* an additional side—ie if the block has two-inch sides, then the strip will be 2+2+2+2+2

=10 inches. Score with a knife along the entire length of the strip ½ inch up from its edge; then score across the strip at each two inch point so that it can be bent into four sides of a square, with one side overlapping. Then cut a small 'v' at each two inch point along the bottom of the ½ inch section so that it can be folded inwards to form a base upon which the block of Plasticine stands when the sides are folded around it, held in place by a rubber band.

A permanent mould-box can be made of wood, with a bottom but no top. Lego bricks make a perfect box, with the bottom row of bricks attached to the base with Sellotape to prevent it being forced out by the weight of its contents.

Press into the Plasticine a cut-down golf tee, or build up a cone-shaped piece of Plasticine leading from the external surface of the mould into the underside of the base of the figure, forming a run-in for the molten metal when the two halves of the mould are matched. Finally, wide of the figure in two of the four corners of the mould, press the rounded end of a pencil or a piece of dowelling, leaving two deep impressions in the Plasticine. When the rubber is poured, the first half of the mould will have two well-raised projections or 'keys' which fit into corresponding holes in the other half of the mould so ensuring that the halves lock accurately.

Silastic RTV mould making rubber has natural release properties for most pattern and casting materials but some do not release readily and when Silicone rubber is poured onto Silicone rubber, as in the two-part mould under construction, a release-agent is essential. So, immediately before pouring the silastomer, paint the sides of the mould-box, the Plasticine floor and the figure itself with releasing-agent—applied very sparingly to the figure to avoid obscuring its definition and preventing a sharp impression. An ideal release-agent is made by mixing five per cent petroleum jelly with 95 per cent white spirit (methylene chloride) then standing the container in hot water; as the white spirit warms up the petroleum jelly dissolves whilst the mixture is stirred. Keep the mixture tightly stoppered when not in use and shake or stir well before applying since it has a slight tendency to separate. If the jelly settles in storage, warm the mixture as before and stir.

Apply the release-agent by dipping, brushing or spraying.

It is sometimes difficult to immediately detect the identity of the impression in a mould. A permanent title can be ingrained in the rubber of the mould by obtaining a reverse-image by typing or writing the name on a piece of paper with carbon-paper inserted *backwards* behind it (ie with shiny side of carbon against reverse of paper). This reversed carbon image, on paper cut to fit, is laid along the inside of the mould-box before the rubber is poured. When the rubber block emerges, permanently engraved on its side will be 'Cuirassier' or whatever.

The importance of thorough mixing of the catalyst and the rubber cannot be over-emphasised; care and thoroughness are required for consistent results. Thoroughly stir Silastic G in the tin before use, because separation may occur if it has been standing for any length of time; agitate the catalyst before use and do not leave it uncovered for prolonged periods of time. Uncoated paper containers are recommended as mixing-containers because they can be thrown away after use to prevent the possibility of contaminating subsequent batches of rubber.

Estimate the amount of rubber needed to completely cover the half embedded pattern by about 13mm—it is better to use too little rather than to mix too much because, once catalyst has been added, the rubber cannot be returned to the can. Pour the desired amount of base liquid rubber into a container and weigh it, then weigh the catalyst in a separate container in the correct proportion of one-tenth that of the base. Pour the catalyst into the container of base liquid rubber and mix them thoroughly, using a stirring rod—the white Silastic G has its own pink catalyst and the catalysed rubber takes on an even pink hue when properly catalysed. Endeavour to avoid trapping excessive air in the rubber during mixing—air bubbles in the mould can be avoided by brushing the initial coat onto the pattern before subsequently topping up the mould.

Slowly pour the catalysed Silastic RTV Silicone Rubber into the mould-box, not directly onto the pattern but allowing it to flow around the figure so avoiding entrapping air, until the model is half covered. Cease pouring for a few minutes to allow the rubber to level off, then resume pouring until the model is covered at its highest point with at least 13mm of silicone rubber. Ensuring that the mould-box is standing level, leave the rubber to cure for a minimum of 24 hours and preferably 72 hours. At the end of the curing-period place the mould-box and its contents in a refrigerator for an hour or so as chilled Plasticine is easier to remove. Gently peel the Plasticine from the rubber block, usually leaving the pattern in the rubber. Next, carefully remove the figure from its rubber half-mould; take great care because the rubber, although reasonably flexible, possesses a certain brittleness which can damage the edge of the impression. Do not use force to remove the pattern from the rubber nor bend it because, when replaced in its cavity, the pattern must fit exactly otherwise each half of the impression will be different.

With a small stiff brush, clean the working surface of the half-mould of any loose particles of rubber or Plasticine and clip away the thin pieces of rubber which may have accumulated around the edges of the impression and the corners and sides of the rubber block.

Replace the pattern and the run-in in their impressions; the half-mould is now placed, impression uppermost, in the mould-box in exactly the same manner as before but the base of the box is silastomer instead of Plasticine. Paint the sides of the mould-box and the interfaces of the mould with release-agent, particularly applying it around the 'keys' as they are prone to stick in the impressions of the second mould half and break off when separating them. Brush a very thin film of release-agent over the figure, not enough to blur its detail. Mix the silastomer and catalyst in their correct proportions; previous experience indicates how much to mix. Pour exactly as before and leave to cure.

When the curing period has elapsed, remove the block of rubber from the mould-box and gently work the two halves apart. Loose filmy strips of rubber may be binding the edges of the interfaces and will need clipping with scissors. The halves separated, remove the pattern gently and clean up mould surfaces as before.

That is the basic way to make a two-part Silastic mould and this is the recommended procedure until the maker has gained sufficient experience to undertake alternative economical methods of manufacture. For example, fabric reinforcement to a mould adds strength whilst requiring less of this rather expensive rubber. To withstand the temperature that will be common to these moulds, something like glass fibre fabric will be required, with an open-weave permitting the Silastic material to freely flow through and achieve a good bond. It can be incorporated at any point in the mould by placing the fabric on the still fluid rubber and then pouring the remainder of the fluid over it; the fabric should not be allowed to contact the pattern because it will interfere with the detail of the impression.

Another method of economising on Silastic rubber is to utilise the rubber of a no-longer-useful mould to make part of the new mould. Pour rubber in the normal manner until the high point of the pattern is just covered and then gently lay the already cut-to-shape slab of the old mould on top of the still liquid rubber, with which it bonds to become part of the mould. Dow Corning, the makers of Silastic RTV rubber, claim that rubber can be reclaimed by cutting a mould up, cleaning with solvent and then grinding to granular form after ensuring that all re-ground material is free of contamination. Only able to be used with the same grade of mould-making rubber, up to 30 per cent (by weight) of reclaimed material can be used in a mould but only as 'backup'; it must never contact the interface of the mould or the pattern.

Damage to a cured Silastic RTV rubber mould can be repaired with additional Silastic RTV rubber by cutting the damaged section away, cleaning the surface with acetone and re-filling by pouring the required amount of catalysed rubber. With care, the actual impression can be repaired by placing the pattern back in its cavity and building up the damaged area with Silastic rubber that has catalysed into Plasticine-like consistency. The makers claim that minor repairs can be carried out by a 'one-component' Silastic RTV rubber such as Silastic 732 RTV and that ripped or torn moulds can be mended with silicone RTV adhesive sealant. Reinforcing fabric placed over the tear will add strength but the detailed surface of the mould cannot be repaired by patching except in the manner described above.

With the current price of Silastic G (including catalyst) at over £3 a pound, Silicone rubber moulds are expensive to construct because, until practical experience is gained, there is an inevitable wastage of materials. It is common sense to nurture successful moulds by methods which substantially lengthen their life. The mould should be conditioned to its high temperature use by heating before use in increments of 77°F (25°C) for half an hour to within 77°F (25°C) of the maximum temperature of the casting material; then maintained for two hours at this top temperature (about 400°F). The life of a mould is lengthened by ensuring that its halves are allowed to cure for a maximum 72 hours at room temperature.

There are no toxicological problems in handling Silastic RTV solutions so far as the skin is concerned, although contact with the eyes may cause temporary discomfort but no irritation and can be alleviated by irrigating the eyes with warm water.

Silastic RTV silicone rubber and catalyst should be stored in closed containers at or below room temperature; their shelf life is about nine months when stored at 75°F and longer in cooler conditions. Silastic RTV Silicone rubber kept beyond its shelf-life may still be usable and in most cases only the curing rate is affected by long storage. If in doubt about the usability of the rubber, make a test using a small amount of rubber with the correct catalyst addition, checking that the curing takes place normally. The catalyst should always be kept in a tightly closed container and never unnecessarily exposed to the air.

When casting with a silicone mould it is necessary for the relatively flexible rubber to be given a rigid back-up shell that holds it in shape when the molten metal is poured in. A wooden box (similar to the mould-box) can be built around the mould, leaving the run-in aperture uppermost; or a similar support can be constructed from Lego. A Plaster of Paris jacket can be poured to surround the rubber mould but this jacket heats up with the mould, making removal a difficult business after each casting operation. Two pieces of hardboard the same size as the mould placed on either side of the rubber and clamped together in a four-part sandwich, with the run-in uppermost, make a satisfactory support.

Before beginning the casting operations, the most important consideration is the metal to be used for the casting—the first and most natural impulse is to find the cheapest possible source, such as old gas pipes or pieces of lead tubing, but they are too soft and will not run into the mould nor will they give other than a soft and ill-defined model. Some metals give the figure a fine definition but at the same time are brittle and very hard to work when cleaning up. Perhaps the most satisfactory and readily available combination is two parts of plumber's solder to one part of tinsmith's solder. A cheaper combination is two parts of ordinary lead to one part of printers' type, usually obtained from a print shop where a considerable surplus of small cuttings is often available for disposal. If the best figures are required then a standard casting alloy can be purchased from a lead supply company or an alloy made from materials available from a die-casting supply house—60 per cent lead, 36 per cent tin, two per cent antimony, one per cent bismuth and one per cent copper.

The container in which the metal is heated can be an old saucepan or a proper cast-iron melting pot, purchased from an ironmongers. A ladle from which the metal is poured will be required and a pair of asbestos (oven) gloves are a good investment.

Before pouring, lightly dust the mould surface with graphite which furnishes an escape route for the gasses forming at the interface of the molten metal and rubber mould, so allowing high quality castings.

Do not let the metal 'boil' for long periods as this makes it 'lazy' and it will not run through the mould so that bayonets and other extremities do not come out. Heat until darker oxides discolour the surface of the silver molten lead which will stay molten in the mould for a few seconds before solidifying. A 'dross' or scum occasionally forms upon the surface of the molten metal in its pot, and has to be skimmed off as it impedes pouring and spoils the casting. By holding the ladle above the pouring hole, the stream of molten metal drops down into the hole and forces its way by its own weight into the many crevices of the impression. As soon as the metal has solidified, open the mould and remove the casting with a pair of pliers. Remember that it is very hot and can inflict an unpleasant burn!

Do not be discouraged if the first castings are imperfect as the mould works best when it has warmed up. Efficient and safe casting is best carried out by using a battery of three moulds, pouring into the first one, then the second and so on, one after the other; then go back and open the first one, remove the figure and clamp the mould together again, do the same with the second one and so on.

Although the makers of Silicone rubber claim that moulds work best when pre-heated there is no doubt that the constant unremitting heat of repeated casting damages them. Perhaps the best results are obtained by allowing a mould to cool between every four or five castings. When the casting session is over, the moulds should be carefully stored away in a box and put in a cool place.

By far the most irritating and arduous part of casting one's own figures is the later stages of 'cleaning-up', filing off the flash attached to the figure and in the undercuts. When the figures are cool, the wedge-shaped run-in is cut off and the more obvious flash gently clipped away with small shears; clean off other unwanted metal and the bottom of the base with files.

The systematic model soldier maker selects the tools required for cleaning-up operations and places them in a line on the table or bench. First comes the snippers, clippers or shears then a selection of ratstail files—rough, round, flat, smooth and knife-edged. Pick up the first casting and the first tool and snip off the obvious flash then do the same to the second figure and so on; then use the second tool on all the figures then the third and so on until they are completed and ready for painting. Castings can be cleaned up by using an electric drill with suitable attachments but a rather fine degree of control is required or else half the figure goes and the casting is ruined!

In conclusion, the amateur model-soldier maker should always bear in mind the mould-making requires patience, but it is well rewarded because 'the better the mould, the better the casting'.

fourteen

Martin Rendall
Carving figures from wood

One of the most rewarding and satisfying modelling techniques, to those who take the time and bother to learn it, is carving figures from wood. Martin Rendall, a professional sculptor, has created many beautiful figures which draw 'ohs!' of admiration wherever they are seen or illustrated. Here he shows how, with the help of a few simple tools and a reasonable modicum of patience, you too can create unique figures of your own from wood.

Wood carving, or whittling (as it is known in America), dates back thousands of years, and through time the fascination of shaping a piece of wood with a blade has brought to light many a budding artist who had not before realised his or her talents. Maybe some of you reading this may have wooden figures or models you have carved in the past, and should you wish to try again, or if this sort of venture is new to you, but you feel inspired, here is the procedure I use, that might assist you in some way.

My first figure is standing straight with his arms close to the body. It is best for beginners to try the less ambitious and not-so active figures, as extended arms and legs on an action model are inclined to snap off if undue pressure is applied by accident, either by holding it too tight or pushing the knife blade too hard. The first subject I tackled, was the Emperor of the Aztec people, called Montezuma, who died in 1519. The type of clothes he wore were both rich and artistic even though he wasn't over-dressed, and his head-dress was a work of art, as were all the decorations used in that age, containing precious stones and gold. As for their beliefs (for the warrior), death in battle or on the sacrificial altar was the ideal way to end this life and enter into a happy eternity with the ranks of the 'Quauhteca', or companions of the eagle, who accompany the sun forever on its travels through the heavens.

Before the carving begins, it is best to have a drawing to work from. You may not consider it necessary, but it is a help to have a drawing to refer to and check measurements and proportions as you go along. A front and side view of your standing figure are needed and you may either trace from pictures or draw free-hand. If the picture you have traced is only the front view, it may help you to (with pencil lines) square up the plan paper into suitable size squares, then using the lines to match up the pro-

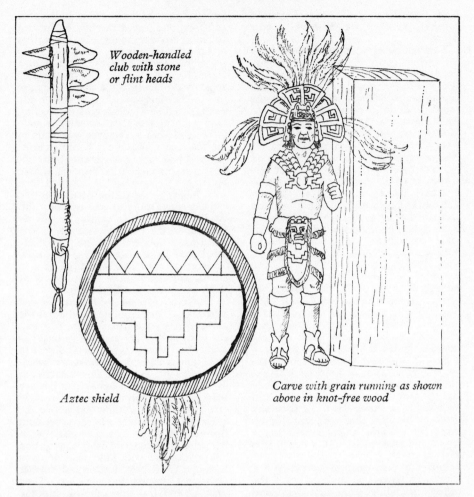

Wooden-handled club with stone or flint heads

Aztec shield

Carve with grain running as shown above in knot-free wood

portions to correspond with your first drawing, draw the side view. Now with front and side view drawn, you are ready to transfer (using carbon paper) the front view on to your block of wood, which should be as near the figure size as possible. To use a large piece of wood for a small figure will give you a lot of unnecessary work cutting it down to size.

Now the wood. To really enjoy carving, you would do well to find a moderate cutting wood, and leave the hard woods alone when just using the tools I mention in this article. If you have a saw mill or timber yard near your locality, don't be afraid to pop in and see if they have any off-cuts to recommend you try. Some of the woods that

carvers used in the past are not always so easy to come by these days, but you never know your luck. I enjoy carving Lime wood, which is a medium cutting wood with a close grain, that will take fine detail carving without breaking. Another nice wood is Jelutong, imported from Malaya, and well worth any trouble you may have getting a piece. Next and getting firmer are Walnut, Pear, Beech and some of the Pine family (not the coarse-grained variety). Some of you may enjoy working on the much softer woods like Obeche or Balsa, but when working on these, it is even more important to use a very sharp blade or the fibres of the wood are inclined to tear instead of cut. Small detail carving may be tricky but you might enjoy it.

Now assuming you have found a suitable piece of wood—back to the figure!

Having traced your front view using the carbon paper on to the wood, you next proceed to saw around as much of the shape as possible. I use a small coping saw, obtainable in most hardware shops, and quite cheap (better still to use a jig-saw or band saw if you know anyone who will let you). Now, with the front shape cut out, and again using the carbon paper, trace the side drawing on to thin cardboard. You then cut the shape out of the cardboard and use it as a stencil, placing it against the side of the block figure and lightly pencilling around the cut-out shape, onto your block figure, giving you a side view to be sawn around as before, which when finished, should leave you with a shaped, square, wooden man.

Now is the time to try your hand at carving, and the knife first needed (or you may prefer to use it all along) is a penknife with a good steel blade. This is for the heavier cut where you can slice and split sections away that are not needed, the blade being thick enough to cope with stubborn slices of wood without snapping. Your first strokes with the blade are to round off the square body and cut away the surplus wood (first) on his right arm, shaping it to lie naturally down by his side, then trim and slightly shape his left arm which is bent at the elbow and forward to hold a shield that will be attached later.

You can then proceed to cut in the chest and taper the angle to meet the throat, rounding the shoulders and shaping in to meet the hair line. The head I leave until later, just forming a very basic shape of the head-dress and blob of a face at this stage. I find it better to finish the body first and then carve a head to match, rather than make a body to fit the head. Next make a shallow cut around the bottom of the skirt then trim the tops of the legs into it, making them narrower than the skirt (this cut-away at this stage need only be about $\frac{1}{16}$ inch deep). Then, remembering at what angle the legs look natural, from thigh to foot, and leaving enough wood for the toes, you can carve away the front of the one leg shaping it to stand at the back of the figure, then proceed to carve his other leg down the back of the knee to the heel of his foot, until this leg looks in a

forward position, then shape in the toes and foot, and round the legs off leaving sufficient wood on to carve leg ornaments and the sandal tops etc.

I enjoy carving a figure by removing a layer of wood all over, then proceeding again to get closer to the shape I require (if you can imagine it). It is rather like seeing a figure which begins by wearing vast quantities of clothes, and as each layer of clothes is removed you start to see the true shape of the figure emerge. When this is applied to carving, however, as you start to reach the required shape, remember to consult your drawing, then (if it helps) pencil in the detail required on your wooden figure and trim in to it. At this stage of the carving a thinner blade than the penknife is most useful, and I use a Stanley knife (No 5900) with a No 5901 shaped blade. These are ideal for cutting thin slices and putting in detail, but don't abuse them by taking thick cuts as they will snap.

The face and head need extra care and attention. Remembering the basic anatomy rules that artists use for drawing, the head should be made as an oval egg shape, but when carving, don't forget to leave enough wood for whatever head-gear you have in mind. For example, as in the Aztec's head-dress, you have a brim or peak, don't cut them away in error, but saw a shallow cut above the eyebrow level, taking the measurement from the chin upwards after referring to the drawing, then cut away the section below your saw cut. This will leave you with the front peak jutting out further than area needed for the face. Then draw a pencil line across the width of the face just below the peak, which is the eyebrow line. Another line drawn down the centre of the intended face gives you a nose guide line, cutting away each side of the nose and just below the eyebrow line until you have reached sufficient depth to give you a prominent nose on the figure. Again check your drawing for the length of nose required then cut away the area between the end of the nose and the chin, leaving a slight bulge of wood to carve the lips in. Next tackle the eye bulges, cheek bones and chin, after which you can see the face shape emerging and I leave it to you to trim and add detail as you see fit, until there is character and human features to satisfy you.

Hands I first shape into oblong blocks

(only just big enough to be in proportion and allow enough wood for detail). These I leave at the end of the arms until I am ready to work on them, at which time, if a closed fist is needed as with the Aztec who holds a war club in the one hand and the shield straps in the other, I carefully drill a hole the size of whatever is to be held, then, either shaping a small piece of dowel or strip of wood just long enough to protrude each side of the hand I am working on, and just tight enough to stay in place through the hole made, I proceed to carve the hands and fingers in detail around the inserted dowel. Carving hands this way, grasping the dowel, gives one a better idea of how thick you want the palms of the hand and the fingers to be. The dowel being so small won't get in the way while you trim all around, then, when the hands are finished, you can discard the dowel, leaving the hands prepared for the weapons you will add at the end of the completed figure, and give the finishing touches. Open hands are carved flat and tapering and have uneven length fingers: one look at your own hands should give you the idea.

The pictures, I hope, will give you an even better idea of progress with the figure, which show some of the stages it went through, to the point of having the bulk of the wood removed and the detail added to the head-dress, fringes of the skirt and decoration on the front and back panels of the skirt, then the carving of the human frame showing a few muscles and down to the feet which were wearing bootie top sandals with the toes in view. All that was then needed was a base to stand on, a shield, carved and painted with an Aztec design, and the war club. I leave it to you to add any item you might think would improve the finished effect.

A quick sanding to remove any rough spots and a coating of shellac to seal the grain (another quick sand, should the shellac make the fibres of the wood stand out), then you are ready for the painting. Most of you will have your own ideas which colours look most effective on this type of figure. Personally, using Humbrol paints, I filled in the broad areas of the head-dress, the skirt and sandals with matt light blue, with a small amount of darker blue design. Front and rear panels of the skirt were matt red fringes, with white and green design

panels. All the raised decorations on the head-dress, arm and leg bracelets, skirt mask and neckwear were in gold paint. Native skin colour was a mixture of brown, sand and a touch of red, which completed my figure.

Now for the more advanced modeller who may have thought the Aztec figure a bit tame, and have perhaps done similar work in the past, this next model is for you, and will require a lot of patience, time and care, plus one or two gouges that, although not absolutely necessary, can be a great help. On this figure I used a $\frac{3}{8}$ inch and a $\frac{1}{4}$ inch slightly curved gouge, then as before that good old standby, the penknife, the coping saw and the Stanley knife. Once again, access to a band saw etc is a great help, although you can use the coping saw as I did (it just takes longer!). For those of you who are not experienced, but willing to have a go, remember that undue pressure applied while holding the figure too firmly, or pushing the blade too hard on an unsupported piece of wood, will snap any of the horse's legs or the man's arms due to their slimness with no support, but should it happen, Evo-Stick wood adhesive (white) will repair the break. Even so, go carefully.

For my horseman model I chose a 'Samurai', the fighting warriors of Japan whom I expect most of you will have heard or know about. The period I picked was called 'The Edo Period' (1603-1867) which presented a choice of very colourful and splendid dress (as do the other periods). To commence, as before, it is best to have a drawing to refer to, and for the horse figure the most important view is the side one as it covers a much wider area with more detail shown than a front view, so again, using the same procedure as for the standing figure, finish your front and side drawing, then trace out the *side* view (using the carbon paper) onto your block of wood. When ready, saw around the shape, then again using the carbon paper and the side drawing, reverse the direction of the horse and place it beside the opposite side of the wood shape. Then draw in the legs of the man on the wood, so each side of the horse has the man's leg positions showing. You can then cut away the area of wood in front of the Samurai's legs and the section behind to the depth shown on the front view drawing, which should leave the Samurai's

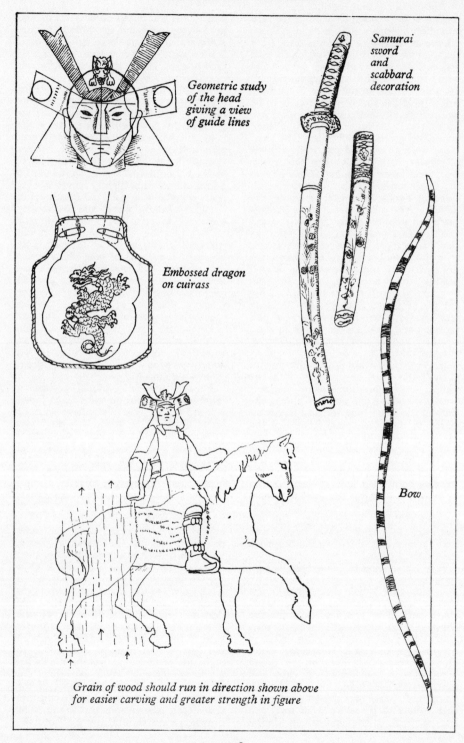

Geometric study
of the head
giving a view
of guide lines

Samurai
sword
and
scabbard
decoration

Embossed dragon
on cuirass

Bow

Grain of wood should run in direction shown above
for easier carving and greater strength in figure

legs sticking out from the horse's sides.

You can then proceed to cut away the section joining the horse's legs (you might find the gouges useful at this stage). Make sure you carve the correct legs away, and don't leave yourself with a horse having two legs raised on the same side! This is an easy mistake to make when you are absorbed in carving, and leaves you speechless when you realise your error later.

With all the legs separated you can shape and round them off, then continue rounding the horse's body and shape into the neck and head. The tail and mane can also be trimmed but at this stage no real detail need be put in. Up till now the man has not been carved at all, and should be still in his block form sitting on the rounded, shaped form of the horse. Now is the time to tackle the Samurai, cutting and shaping his knees into his waist, taking the surplus wood away in front of the chest section, then shaping the arms, one which is up ready to grasp the reins at a later stage, and the other arm by his side, to hold a bow on completion of the figure. The Stanley knife comes into play now the rounding off is done, and it is time to remove the final layers of wood around the head and hat, and put in the face features, remembering that the Japanese have high cheek bones and very slightly slanted eyes.

Next the armour and the lacing is cut in, then the dragon embossed on the cuirass, on to the armoured sleeves, shinguards and feet. The horse detail can be carved in now, the muscles, the head, ears and yes, nostrils, mouth, etc; tiger skin, saddle and hair strands. When you are satisfied with your carving, apply the shellac after smoothing off with fine sandpaper, then, as before, if the shellac raises the fibres of wood, lightly sand again. This completes the basic figure. Now come the accessories, carving the shoulder-guards, sword (katana) and the short sword out of wood. The arrows were bamboo, split and shaped, with feather flights made from real feathers (obtained from the bottom of the budgerigar cage—during his moulting period. Please don't pull the feathers out). These were cut to size, split with a razor blade and glued onto the shafts, as with real arrows. When the glue set I trimmed down the feathers to suit. I used stiff metal strip to make the helmet crest and the curved wings

(Fukigayeshi) decorated with cut-out discs, cut from a thinner metal foil (toothpaste tube that was discarded). This was also used to make Japanese style stirrups.

Lacing and cords were either plaited fuse wire painted, or embroidery silks. The cuirass I edged with twisted wire to give a rope decoration, and again used it wherever I thought looked most effective. Next a base was attached, as I could not find a suitable style in the shops (I was looking for the type of Chinese stand that one sometimes sees in second-hand shops). I made my own from a flat piece of wood that I slightly shaped and cut about to resemble bases seen in the past.

The accessories were attached to the Samurai at this stage, the horse trappings I left until the horse was painted, as were the bow and the reins. The painting of the model can be started in earnest now (I had applied a touch of paint in odd areas for undercoat or to get an idea of colour but now the correct colours were used). You may have in mind your own colour scheme for the painting so I won't dwell too·much on my efforts, other than to say that the horse was painted in brown tones using Rowney Cryla colour, with black mane and tail. The blending of these colours were also used on the tiger skin.

Humbrol paint was used on the Samurai, painting the metal work in gloss black, gunmetal and steel with gold trimmings, while the armour plate lacings which were carved into the figure were coloured in matt yellow, red, black and light brown. Gloss red was used on the swords and parts of the helmet then, when dry, decorated with gold. The figure's stockings were duck-egg blue with dark blue shoes, and his armoured sleeves (Kote) red with fine gold and black designs.

For those of you who tackled either of these projects, there will be two schools of thought, the ones who ask 'why ever did I start' and those who say 'it turned out better than I hoped'. In either case, I only hope you found a certain element of fun in the achievement of creating something out of a block of wood, and worth all the effort.

Measurements of these models for those interested: height of the Aztec 6½ inches not counting feathers (real feathers taken from a coloured feather duster). Height of Samurai 7¼ inches by 7 inches long.

appendix

Compiled by the Editor
Model figure suppliers

The following list of manufacturers and suppliers cannot hope to be comprehensive because new names are cropping up all the time while old ones disappear. However, it includes the addresses of all those manufacturers I was able to verify at the time of going to press.

Most manufacturers and suppliers can provide catalogues and price lists on request, although some of the catalogues are fairly expensive. When writing to any manufacturer please remember to enclose a stamped, self-addressed envelope for a reply. Remember also, when ordering by mail, that although the majority of suppliers practice a reasonably fast delivery service, seasonal demands and availability of stocks can often cause delays. In general, don't start worrying for six weeks or so.

Finally, and most important, NEVER send cash with any order unless you mail it by Registered Post. Not only is it illegal, but your chances of ever seeing either the requested model(s) or your money back are extremely remote. Always send crossed cheques or Postal Orders, or International Money Orders if applying for goods from abroad.

Not all model shops stock all ranges, for obvious reasons. In cases where a shop specialises in a particular line, this is noted in brackets after the name. The fact that other manufacturers' products are not noted does not necessarily mean they are not stocked (for example, a firm may specialise in, say, Hinchliffe—but also stock Lasset, Lamming, Warrior and many others). All suppliers listed run a mail order service for individual customers, but some manufacturers (for example, Airfix) do not. Manufacturers are indicated by an asterisk *.

Finally, while every care has been taken to check the bona fides of the firms in the following list, neither the publishers, authors, editor or printers of this book can accept any responsibility for disputes which may arise.

Airfix Products Limited* Haldane Place, Garratt Lane, London SW18 4NB (00/HO and 1:32 scale polythene, 54mm and 1:12 scale polystyrene).

Argyle Models 247 Argyle Street, Glasgow C2, and 26 South Mall, Birmingham Shopping Centre (Bugle & Guidon 54mm metal).

Armour Accessories* 3 Castle Street, Dover (1:35 scale plastic).

Armoury, The 1 Fisher Road, Stoke, Plymouth PL2 3BA (Brundick 54mm metal kits).

Beatties 10 The Broadway, Southgate, London N14 6PN (Airfix and Tamiya etc).

Berwick, Ernest 11A Newland Street, Kettering, Northants (Airfix and Tamiya etc).

Block, James 5 Wurth Place, Chifley 2606, Canberra, Australia (Historex, Helmet, Miniature Figurines, Hinchliffe etc).

BMW Models 327-329 Haydons Road, Wimbledon, London SW19 (Aurora knights, Airfix, Historex, Hinchliffe).

Bowler, Leslie 126 New Cross Road, London SE14 (Airfix etc).

Bridle Models 2 Bridle Parade, Bridle Road, Shirley, Croydon CR0 8HA (Historex, Lasset, Sanderson, Minot, Garrison, Hinchliffe, Trophy, Stadden and Series 77).

Burnaby Hobbies 5221 Rumble Street, Burnaby 1, B.C., Canada (Airfix, Hinchliffe, Series 77, Stadden).

Colberre 48 Station Road, West Drayton, Middlesex UB7 7DB (Minot, Garrison, Lasset, Hinchliffe etc).

Empire Military Miniatures* 33 Marsh Ave, Dronfield, Nr Sheffield (54mm metal).

Ensign Miniatures* 5 Market Place, Woburn, Milton Keynes, MK17 9PZ (54mm metal).

Greenwood & Ball* 61 Westbury Street, Thornaby on Tees, Teesside (Own 54mm plus Lasset, Sanderson, Cameo, Garrison). (USA—Coulter-Bennett Ltd, 12158 Hamlin Street, North Hollywood, California 91606.)

Guard House, The* 6 Cavendish Road, Liverpool L23 6XB (54mm metal kits).

Guard Room, The 24 The Saltisford, Warwick (Most makes).

Hales, A. A. PO Box 33, Hinckley, Leics (Distributors for Bandai 1:48 figures etc).

Harrow The Model Shop, 31 St Ann's Road, Harrow, Middlesex (Garrison and Hinchliffe).

Hazlewood Miniatures* Royal Arcade, Leicester (54mm metal).

Helmet Products* Betchworth, Surrey (54mm polythene/polystyrene kits, some containing wool and fabric for uniform details, some metal-plated parts).

Hinchliffe Models* Meltham, Huddersfield, HD7 3NX (25, 54 and 75mm metal).

Hinton Hunt* 27 Camden Passage, London N1 (20 and 54mm metal).

Historex Agents 3 Castle Street, Dover

(Distributors for Historex 54mm plastic kits and Armour Accessories: South Africa—Victors Hobbies, 70 Grenville Ave, Savoy Estate, Johannesburg; Australia—Zimbler Pty, 9 Carson Street, Kew, Victoria 3101; New Zealand—Bymodels, PO Box 3037, Forbury, Dunedin).

Hobby Supplies 540 High Road, Chiswick, London W4 5RG (Most makes).

Holt Military Models Holt House, Caswell Bay, Swansea, Glam (Hinchliffe).

HQ 1A Craven Passage, Charing Cross, London WC2 (Most makes).

Stan Johansen Miniatures* 41-44 Ridge Road, Maugatuck, Conn 06770, USA (30mm metal).

Imperial Modellings 7 St John Street, Lichfield, Staffs WS13 6NU (Ensign 54mm metal).

Jones Bros 56-62 Turnham Green Terrace, Chiswick, London W4 (Airfix etc).

Kemplay, Peter Framlingham, Woodbridge, Suffolk (Spencer-Smith, Tradition, Stadden, Lamming).

Kingston Mail Order Company 1111 Hedon Road, Hull HU9 5DX (Hinchliffe and Historex).

Kirk Miniature Figures 3 Wynfield Road, Leicester (54mm metal and 1:300).

Kohnstam, Richard 13-15A High Street, Hemel Hempstead, Herts (Distributors for Tamiya figures and vehicles).

Laing, Peter* 11 Bounds Oak Way, Southborough, Tunbridge Wells, Kent TN4 0UB (15mm metal).

Lamming Miniatures* 45 Wenlock Street, Hull HU3 1DA (25mm metal).

Leeds Model Soldier Centre 25 Merrion Street, Leeds 2.

Lippett & Son* 46 The Old High Street, Folkestone, Kent CT20 1RN (Lippett Figures, 90mm metal plus others).

Mainly Military 103 Walsall Road, Lichfield, Staffs (Most makes).

Men o' War* 52 Blenheim Drive, Welling, Kent DA16 3LY (90mm metal).

Michael's Models 646-648 High Road, North Finchley, London N12 0NL.

Militaria* 103 The Quadrangle, 2800 Routh Street, Dallas, Texas 75201, USA (54mm metal).

Militaria Antiques 225 Market Street, Hyde, Cheshire (Most makes).

Miniature Figurines* 28/32 Northam Road, Southampton SO2 0PA (USA—Miniature Figurines, Box P, Pine Plains, New York 12567). (5, 15, 25 and 30mm metal.)

Minot* 20 Watling Street, Elstree, Herts (30 and 54mm metal).

Model Centre 337 Bury Road, Tonge Fold, Bolton (Hinchliffe and Historex).

Model Figures & Hobbies Lower Balloo Road, Groomsport, Co Down, N.I. BT19 2LU (SEGOM 25 and 54mm acetate, Jackboot 54mm metal, Acorn 80mm metal damsels).

Model Hobby Consortium 363 Lewisham High Street, London SE13 (Historex, Lasset, Hinchliffe, Series 77 etc).

Modelmark 8 Mighell Avenue, Redbridge, Ilford, Essex (Mainly Airfix etc but some useful items).

Models & Figurines 436 Military Road, Mosman 2088, Australia.

Model-time* 6 St George's Walk, Croydon, Surrey CR0 1YG (54mm metal).

Old Guard, The 30 Baker Street, London W1M 2DS (Old Guard 54mm figures and kits).

Old Soldier, The 14 James Street, St Catharines, Ontario L2R 5B8, Canada (Most makes—mail order in North America only).

Operation Militaire 11 Essenden Road, Belvedere, Kent (See Starcast Miniatures).

Oxford Model Centre 94 St Clements, Oxford OX4 1AR (Most makes).

Phoenix Model Developments* The Square, Earls Barton, Northampton (Les Higgins 20mm and metal 54mm kits).

Ren-models 63 Fitzroy Street, Cambridge CB1 1HF (Mainly Airfix etc, also Hinchliffe).

Risley, Imrie* Copiague, NY 11726, USA (54mm and 1:24 scale metal).

Rose Miniatures* 15 Llanover Road, London SE18 3ST (25, 30 and 54mm metal).

Rye Stamp and Hobby Shop 190 Rye Lane, Peckham, London SE15 4NF (Miniature Figurines).

Seagull Model 15 Exhibition Road, London SW7 (Most makes, including Jac and some unusual items on occasion).

Sentry Box, The* Basement B3, 112 Holland Road, London W14 8BD (120mm and 54mm metal).

Series 77* 25 Britannia Drive, Gravesend, Kent DA12 4RP (Distributed in USA by Coulter-Bennett Ltd, 12158 Hamlin Street, North Hollywood, California 91606, and in Canada by Wellington Barracks Miniatures, Postal Station L, Box 58231, Vancouver, BC).

Skytrex 28 Church Street, Wymeswold, Loughborough, Leics (Mainly 1:300 scale).

Soldier Shop, The 1013 Madison Avenue, New York, NY 10021, USA (Imrie-Risley, Historex, Cavalier, Old Guard, Superior, Stadden, Bugle & Guidon, Labayen, Lasset, Victory, Series 77, Valiant etc).

Soldier World PO Box 381, Altoona, Pennsylvania, USA 16603 (C & C 20mm, Bussler and Monarch 54mm).

Soldiers 36 Kennington Road, London SE1 (Cavalier and Heroics plus most other makes in all scales, and old Britains).

Spencer-Smith Miniatures* 66 Longmeadow, Frimley, Camberley, Surrey (30mm plastic).

Sports & Hobbies 25 Market Way, The Tricorn, Portsmouth, Hants (Springwood 25mm plastics).

Squadron Shop, The 23500 John R. Hazel Park, Michigan 48030, USA (America's largest model concern: Valiant, Old Guard, Cavalier, Imrie-Risley, etc).

Starcast Miniatures* 11 Essenden Road, Belvedere, Kent (Mainly 1:300 scale).

Thomson, Ian R. F. 54 Upland Road, South Croydon, Surrey CR2 6RE (H.R., Imrie-Risley and Britains metal).

Tin Soldier, The 57 Church Road, Tranmere, Birkenhead L42 5LD (Most makes).

Tradition* 188 Piccadilly, London W1 (Tradition 25mm, Stadden 30 and 54mm, old Britains and Elastolin, militaria etc).

Train Shop Supermarket 4 Bertram Road, Bradford BD8 7LN (Most makes and scales).

Trophy Miniatures* 1 Adlington Road, Oadby, Leicester (Elite Figures).

Under Two Flags 4 St Christopher's Place, Wigmore Street, London W1 (Most makes).

Wakefield Model Railway Centre 260 Dewsbury Road, Wakefield (Most makes).

Wall Models 373 High Street North, Manor Park, London E12 6PG (Miniature Figurines and Hinchliffe).

Warrior Metal Miniatures* 23 Grove Road, Leighton Buzzard, Beds LU7 8SF (25mm metal).

Weiner Metallfigurinen* 1090 Wien, Gussenbauergasse 5-7, Austria (54mm metal).

Westby Products* East Keswick, Nr Leeds, LS17 9EH (Home tin-casting kits and moulds).

Wyvern Models 25 Godwin Close, Mount Hill, Halstead, Essex (Rose, Lasset, Sanderson, Garrison).

Last but not least, if you intend to take modelling miniature figures seriously, you should certainly consider joining the British Model Soldier Society, which has branches and holds meetings, auctions, lectures, competitions, demonstrations and exhibitions all over Britain. For full details write to: Mr J. Ruddle, Hon Sec, BMSS, 22 Priory Gardens, Hampton, Middlesex.